Couchbase Essentials

Harness the power of Couchbase to build flexible and scalable applications

John Zablocki

BIRMINGHAM - MUMBAI

Couchbase Essentials

First published: February 2015

Production reference: 1200215

Published by Packt Publishing Ltd.
Livery Place
35 Livery Street
Birmingham B3 2PB, UK.

ISBN 978-1-78439-449-3

www.packtpub.com

Credits

Author
John Zablocki

Reviewers
Roy Enjoy
Philip Hanson
Aleksandar Mićović
Chris Wilkinson

Commissioning Editor
Pramila Balan

Acquisition Editors
Richard Gall
Richard Brookes-Bland

Content Development Editor
Kirti Patil

Technical Editors
Shashank Desai
Rikita Poojari

Copy Editor
Vikrant Phadke

Project Coordinator
Nidhi Joshi

Proofreaders
Safis Editing
Maria Gould
Paul Hindle

Indexer
Rekha Nair

Production Coordinator
Nilesh R. Mohite

Cover Work
Nilesh R. Mohite

About the Author

John Zablocki is the director of information technology at EF High School Exchange Year in Cambridge, Massachusetts, USA. Previously, he worked at Couchbase Inc. as a developer advocate, maintaining the .NET SDK and delivering training to customers and users alike. John is the author of O'Reilly's *Orchard CMS*. He is a frequent presenter at community events and has run Code Camps and user groups. He holds a Master's degree in computer science from Rensselaer at Hartford, where he became an enthusiast of open source technology. John can be approached online at http://about.me/johnzablocki and around Cambridge with his daughter, Mary Katherine; his dog, Lady; and his Fender Jaguar.

About the Reviewers

Roy Enjoy started to improve his geeky skills with a Commodore 64, some QBasic, and lots of Boulderdash. Then, the Internet exploded after bulletin board systems. Since it is always a shovel man who gets paid first in a gold rush, he decided to thrive within web technologies.

After finishing courses in a couple of IT-oriented schools and playing with a large number of different languages, frameworks, and databases, he worked in different parts of the world, including India, Australia, Turkey, the Netherlands, and Serbia. He is currently living in Australia, and he is trying to learn 3D animation / VFX programming and computer-generated imagery these days.

As an open source evangelist, Roy maintains an API documentation and source code search engine for the Python programming language, named pydoc.net, which is also an open source project.

Philip Hanson is a full-time professional software developer with a diverse background ranging from micro-ISV SaaS to capital-e enterprise development. He continues to experiment with new languages, techniques, and approaches to solve the world's problems.

Aleksandar Mićović started programming at the age of 12. Many years later, he graduated from the University of Toronto with a degree in computer science. Today, he's a professional software engineer and consultant in Belgrade, Serbia, with clients spanning across the globe. When he's not working, he enjoys cooking, reading, and traveling. You can contact him at http://aleksandarmicovic.com/.

Chris Wilkinson has spent years in the software development industry after attaining a degree in Computer Games Programming at the University of Teesside. After making the move into business IT upon leaving the university, Chris has worked all over the world, developing Java applications for businesses in many verticals, including finance, aerospace, and the public sector. Specialized in web and big data technologies, Chris now manages the development team for Askaris Information Technology, a new start-up business developing software for some of the largest oilfield drilling companies in the world.

www.PacktPub.com

Support files, eBooks, discount offers, and more

For support files and downloads related to your book, please visit www.PacktPub.com.

Did you know that Packt offers eBook versions of every book published, with PDF and ePub files available? You can upgrade to the eBook version at www.PacktPub.com and as a print book customer, you are entitled to a discount on the eBook copy. Get in touch with us at service@packtpub.com for more details.

At www.PacktPub.com, you can also read a collection of free technical articles, sign up for a range of free newsletters and receive exclusive discounts and offers on Packt books and eBooks.

https://www2.packtpub.com/books/subscription/packtlib

Do you need instant solutions to your IT questions? PacktLib is Packt's online digital book library. Here, you can search, access, and read Packt's entire library of books.

Why subscribe?

- Fully searchable across every book published by Packt
- Copy and paste, print, and bookmark content
- On demand and accessible via a web browser

Free access for Packt account holders

If you have an account with Packt at www.PacktPub.com, you can use this to access PacktLib today and view 9 entirely free books. Simply use your login credentials for immediate access.

Table of Contents

Preface

Not too long ago, I was fortunate enough to have worked for Couchbase Inc. with the developer solutions team. In my role as a developer advocate, I had two primary responsibilities: maintaining the Couchbase .NET SDK and training Couchbase users on how to develop for Couchbase Server.

During my tenure on the SDK team, I worked with hundreds of developers around the world who were using Couchbase Server for a wide variety of solutions. Some were using Couchbase Server for its distributed caching abilities, while others needed a model that could support near-real-time analytics over a flexible schema. I was always impressed with Couchbase Server's ability to handle such a vast number of development scenarios.

Through the countless meetings I had with the development community and customers alike, it became clear to me that NoSQL is far from a technology fad. Along with cloud computing and mobile services, NoSQL has become a part of the fabric from which modern applications are woven.

As with relational databases before them, NoSQL databases such as Couchbase Server are quickly nearing the "required knowledge" status for application developers. Modern applications that need to reach a massive scale or require greater data model flexibility have found success with non-relational systems.

It is a tremendous opportunity to be able to share my experience at Couchbase with you, the reader. This is an exciting technology, and this book contains the tools you need to get started with Couchbase development.

What this book covers

Chapter 1, Getting Comfortable with Couchbase, introduces Couchbase Server and provides details on obtaining and installing it. It also walks you through setting up Couchbase Server for the first time.

Chapter 2, Using Couchbase CRUD Operations, provides an overview of basic Couchbase Server operations. Basic SDK usage is demonstrated while exploring the various CRUD API methods.

Chapter 3, Creating Secondary Indexes with Views, explains in detail the programming model of MapReduce. After this exploration, the basics of using MapReduce within Couchbase Server are explored.

Chapter 4, Advanced Views, explores common view patterns for Couchbase development, following on the previous chapter's discussion of MapReduce.

Chapter 5, Introducing N1QL, introduces the prerelease Couchbase query language, N1QL.

Chapter 6, Designing a Schema-less Data Model, discusses many of the design options that must be considered when building Couchbase Server applications. Both key/value and document schemas are covered.

Chapter 7, Creating a To-do App with Couchbase, provides an overview on how to convert Couchbase Server to a basic to-do application.

Appendix, Couchbase SDKs, contains a brief introduction to the official Couchbase SDKs, including installation and basic usage.

What you need for this book

In order to follow along with the examples in this book, you will need to install Couchbase Server 3.0.x. Installer packages are available for Windows, Mac OS X, and multiple Linux distributions. Couchbase Server comes in both Community and Enterprise editions, and either will work.

The SDK examples shown in this book mostly use the .NET and Couchbase Server SDKs, though any SDK can be used. To try out the SDK samples, you will need to have a development environment for your chosen language and the SDK itself. Details on where to obtain and install both the server and the clients are provided early in the book.

Who this book is for

This book is for those application developers who want greater flexibility and scalability for their software. Whether you are familiar with other NoSQL databases or have used only relational systems, this book will provide you with enough background for you to proceed at your own pace. If you are new to NoSQL document databases, the design discussions and introductory material will give you the information you need to get started with Couchbase.

Conventions

In this book, you will find a number of text styles that distinguish between different kinds of information. Here are some examples of these styles and explanations of their meanings.

Code words in text, database table names, folder names, filenames, file extensions, pathnames, dummy URLs, user input, and Twitter handles are shown as follows: "To update an existing document, we use the `replace` operation."

A block of code is set as follows:

```
function(doc, meta) {
  emit(meta.id, null);
}
```

When we wish to draw your attention to a particular part of a code block, the relevant lines or items are set in bold:

```
function(doc, meta) {
  if (doc.type == "beer") {
    emit(null, null);
  }
}
```

Any command-line input or output is written as follows:

```
./cbq-engine-couchbase http://localhost:8091
```

New terms and **important words** are shown in bold. Words that you see on the screen, for example, in menus or dialog boxes, appear in the text like this: "Brewery documents in the **beer-sample** bucket contain address information."

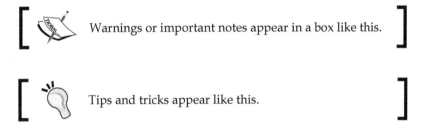

Warnings or important notes appear in a box like this.

Tips and tricks appear like this.

Reader feedback

Feedback from our readers is always welcome. Let us know what you think about this book—what you liked or disliked. Reader feedback is important for us as it helps us develop titles that you will really get the most out of.

To send us general feedback, simply e-mail feedback@packtpub.com, and mention the book's title in the subject of your message.

If there is a topic that you have expertise in and you are interested in either writing or contributing to a book, see our author guide at www.packtpub.com/authors.

Customer support

Now that you are the proud owner of a Packt book, we have a number of things to help you to get the most from your purchase.

Downloading the example code

You can download the example code files from your account at http://www.packtpub.com for all the Packt Publishing books you have purchased. If you purchased this book elsewhere, you can visit http://www.packtpub.com/support and register to have the files e-mailed directly to you.

Errata

Although we have taken every care to ensure the accuracy of our content, mistakes do happen. If you find a mistake in one of our books—maybe a mistake in the text or the code—we would be grateful if you could report this to us. By doing so, you can save other readers from frustration and help us improve subsequent versions of this book. If you find any errata, please report them by visiting http://www.packtpub.com/submit-errata, selecting your book, clicking on the **Errata Submission Form** link, and entering the details of your errata. Once your errata are verified, your submission will be accepted and the errata will be uploaded to our website or added to any list of existing errata under the Errata section of that title.

To view the previously submitted errata, go to https://www.packtpub.com/books/content/support and enter the name of the book in the search field. The required information will appear under the **Errata** section.

Piracy

Piracy of copyrighted material on the Internet is an ongoing problem across all media. At Packt, we take the protection of our copyright and licenses very seriously. If you come across any illegal copies of our works in any form on the Internet, please provide us with the location address or website name immediately so that we can pursue a remedy.

Please contact us at `copyright@packtpub.com` with a link to the suspected pirated material.

We appreciate your help in protecting our authors and our ability to bring you valuable content.

Questions

If you have a problem with any aspect of this book, you can contact us at `questions@packtpub.com`, and we will do our best to address the problem.

1
Getting Comfortable with Couchbase

Couchbase Server has quickly emerged as one of the leading NoSQL databases. Known for powering apps and sites such as Viber, PayPal, LinkedIn, and eBay, Couchbase Server easily serves up terabytes to petabytes of data. Whether used as a distributed cache or a document database, Couchbase Server has become a significant contributor to the growth of the Internet as a whole.

Long before the term NoSQL started to grace the pages of blogs, tech journals, and investor balance sheets, a technology called **Memcached** was providing life support for relational databases. As these systems attempted to reach the scale demanded by modern, Internet-based applications, it was clear that Memcached could help. Still widely used today, Memcached is a distributed key/value store used to provide a caching layer for applications.

Some of the developers on the open source Memcached project saw the potential to take the system beyond a simple cache. They introduced new features such as a binary protocol, better cluster management, and most importantly, persistence. This new and durable offshoot of Memcached became known as **Membase**. A company of the same name was formed to support the project (it is still open source) and provide customers with support in their production environments.

Membase quickly gained popularity with developers who needed massive scalability. From start-ups to stalwarts, this new database was becoming one of the disruptive technologies that would forever change the way applications store data. Around the same time, developers were starting to demand more flexibility from their databases. A seemingly infinite number of web applications were built using **Object Relational Mappers (ORM)** such as **ActiveRecord**, **Hibernate**, and **SQLAlchemy**.

ORMs attempt to simplify the object-to-relational mapping problems often associated with working with a highly normalized database. The basic problem is that the relational model does not always look like an object-oriented model. ORMs hide the underlying data model from the application layer, often by way of a significant amount of configuration. ORMs also provide relational databases with a new lifeline.

One open source project that attempted to solve the object-to-relational mapping problem by doing away with the relational side of things was **CouchDB**. The developers of CouchDB built a database that, in their own words, was for developers and by developers. Tables, columns, and rows were replaced by documents stored as **JSON**. The net result was a system that stored data in structures similar to those found in the application layer.

Eventually, as both Membase and CouchDB matured, the developers of both systems came together for what is one of the most important chocolate-meets-peanut-butter moments in database history. The extremely scalable and reliable Membase would eventually be married to the ever-flexible and developer-friendly CouchDB. Each database would take part of its maiden name in the merger, which was called **Couchbase**.

Today, Couchbase is responsible for developing and supporting **Couchbase Server**. The combined products still remain open source but are no longer tied to their parent projects. While many of the features of Couchbase were inspired by CouchDB and Memcached, the code is anything but a "copy-and-paste" from the parent projects. Make no mistake about it! Couchbase is a standalone product optimized to be better than two otherwise great projects.

The NoSQL landscape

In the crowded market of NoSQL databases, Couchbase Server is one of the dominant players. Its performance sets the bar high for its competitors. The rich feature set of Couchbase Server also sets a new standard for what is expected from NoSQL databases. As NoSQL is still a nascent field, Couchbase Server seems destined to influence its future.

All relational databases tend to be the same animal. Whether you're using SQL Server or MySQL, you could expect to find the same basic set of features. You store your data in rows with strictly defined columns inside a table. You then modify your data using SQL's INSERT and UPDATE statements. You retrieve your data using SQL queries. In contrast, NoSQL databases vary wildly from one system to the next. However, there are some features you would expect to find across various NoSQL taxonomies.

Perhaps the most common feature in NoSQL databases is the lack of an imposed structure on your data. While in practice, structures tend to be defined by your application layer, it is permissible that your NoSQL records are like snowflakes—no two records are the same. This flexibility has made NoSQL databases popular with developers, who no longer have to work within the constraints of a relational schema and ORMs.

Another feature (or lack of a feature) that you could expect to find in NoSQL databases is the lack of explicit **ACID** transactions. In other words, you won't be able to wrap a series of insertions or updates within a transaction. However, this does not mean that ACID properties are not supported in NoSQL databases.

Atomicity is widely supported in NoSQL databases. Partial writes are not possible. Either an entire record is written or nothing is written. **Consistency** in NoSQL ranges from eventual (delayed) consistency to strict consistency. **Isolation** is implicit, which means that a read will never return values from an update in progress. Like consistency, **durability** varies within NoSQL databases and is generally tunable.

The importance of full ACID compliance in NoSQL is somewhat diminished. Often, the need for transactions is dictated by the relational model, where related data is stored in one or more tables. In NoSQL databases, it is common to write related data to a single structure or record. In other words, a single NoSQL update or insertion might require several updates or inserts in the relational world.

This modeling difference also reduces the need for features such as joins or strict referential integrity. When records are stored in a denormalized fashion, a single query may bring back the required object graph.

Of course, it's likely that you will still need to make use of relational concepts in your NoSQL data model. Full denormalization is often impractical in NoSQL. In these cases, the applications that consume the data face an increased burden of being responsible for handling the details that a relational database typically would have dealt with.

Beyond these basic features, NoSQL systems tend to become more and more disparate. Instead, you will be more likely to find similar features between databases in the same NoSQL category. For example, CouchDB and MongoDB are both document stores. While they are fundamentally very different databases, they are more similar to each other than either of them is to a graph database such as **Neo4j** or a column database such as **Cassandra**. In the next section, I'll discuss the different categories of NoSQL databases and describe how Couchbase fits into the big picture.

NoSQL taxonomies

There are many different categories of NoSQL database. A broad definition of NoSQL might consider everything from XML databases to cloud-based BLOB storage as parts of the NoSQL landscape. However, in practice only a few NoSQL databases are widely used, with the vast majority of developer mind share belonging to only two categories, key/value and document stores.

Key/value stores are popular because of their simplicity. Records are stored and retrieved via a key much like programmers use hash tables or dictionary structures to store data in the memory. These systems tend to be highly performant.

Document stores are arguably the most popular of NoSQL databases, driven primarily by the flexibility they offer. Documents are typically stored in a JSON or JSON-like structure. JSON, being a notation for describing object graphs, is a natural fit for object-oriented applications.

While nearly all popular NoSQL databases fall into one category or another, Couchbase is both a key/value and a document store. Records are written to and read from Couchbase using a key/value API. When those records are stored as JSON documents, Couchbase provides document indexing, allowing queries on arbitrary properties in the document structure.

Importantly, Couchbase does not sacrifice features to achieve its duplicity. Though it might seem that such a hybrid system would necessarily be lacking in either its key/value or document capabilities, Couchbase feels complete. As a key/value store, Couchbase offers a rich API based on its Membase heritage. As a document store, Couchbase supports the most important features from its "pure document relative" — CouchDB.

Two data storage models also provide developers with a great deal of flexibility. Applications may be optimized using different approaches for different features; for example, a social game might make use of Couchbase's key/value interface to achieve scaling when collecting or serving vast amount of data. That same application could then use the document interface to retrieve aggregate statistics on players.

Installing Couchbase

There are two editions of Couchbase available for download — **Community** and **Enterprise**. While both editions are largely the same, there are two key differences. The Community Edition is free to use for development and in your production systems. However, there is no guarantee that patches (critical or small) will be made to this build in a timely manner. This edition is intended primarily for development, or for those developers who are okay with relying on free support (that is, the Couchbase forums).

The Couchbase Server Enterprise Edition requires the acceptance of an **End User License Agreement** (**EULA**), with the user agreeing to install it on no more than two production nodes. Use of more than two nodes requires the purchase of a support license. There are a variety of support levels available. Enterprise Edition also receives priority patches and new features ahead of the Community Edition. It is recommended for use in mission-critical systems.

For the examples in this book, there are no meaningful differences between the two editions. As such, we'll use the Community Edition. How you install Couchbase Server will depend on your operating system. Once it is installed, maintaining and developing the server is generally the same experience on both Windows and Linux.

To get started, open your browser and go to `http://www.couchbase.com/download`. Here, you'll find the latest binaries. At the time of writing this book, the latest Enterprise Edition is 2.5.1 and the latest Community Edition is 2.2.0.

Installing Couchbase on Linux

The Couchbase team maintains 32-bit and 64-bit builds for Ubuntu, CentOS, and Red Hat Linux. After downloading the package on Ubuntu, run the following command to install it:

```
sudodpkg -icouchbase-server-enterprise_2.2.0_x86_64.deb
```

For CentOS or Red Hat installation, run this command:

```
sudo rpm --install couchbase-server-enterprise_2.2.0_x86_64.rpm
```

Installing Couchbase on Windows

For Windows 7, Windows 8, and Windows Server, there is a setup program. Simply download the installer, run the `.exe` file, and follow the steps of the wizard. When you install Couchbase on a Windows machine, you'll see the following prompt:

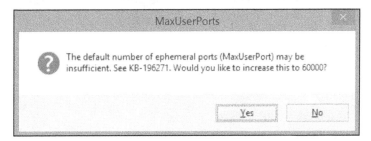

Ephemeral port warning

By default, the highest port number that TCP may assign to an application requesting a user port is 5000 on Windows systems. This value is generally sufficient for development purposes, but in production deployments, Couchbase requires a greater number. For the purpose of this book, leaving your default settings as they are is safe.

Installing Couchbase on Mac OS X

Finally, if you're developing on a Mac, there is a development-only build available. After downloading the Mac package, double-click to unzip it. Then drag the contents into your Applications directory. For obvious reasons, the Mac release is for development only.

Ports

Couchbase Server is constructed using a series of components, each requiring access to a different port. It's common to encounter errors when trying to use Couchbase for the first time, due to blocked ports. You're more likely to have fewer port restrictions on your development machine than on your production servers, but it's still important to make sure you have at least ports 8091, 8092, 11210, and 11211 open. Running a cluster requires more port access, but for development, you'll need to have the web admin accessible (8091) and the API and client endpoint ports open (8092, 11210, and 11211).

Running Couchbase for the first time

One feature that really sets Couchbase apart from the other NoSQL databases is its administrative interface. When you install Couchbase, you also get this powerful web app to manage your server. Moreover, the admin tool is simply a wrapper over a **RESTful** management API supported by the server. In other words, any action you can perform with the admin GUI can also be performed via your favorite DevOps tools.

You can get to the Couchbase Server web admin by opening your browser and going to `http://localhost:8091`. If you've just completed installing Couchbase, there may be a brief delay between the startup of the server and the startup of the admin. Refresh a couple of times, and you should see something like this:

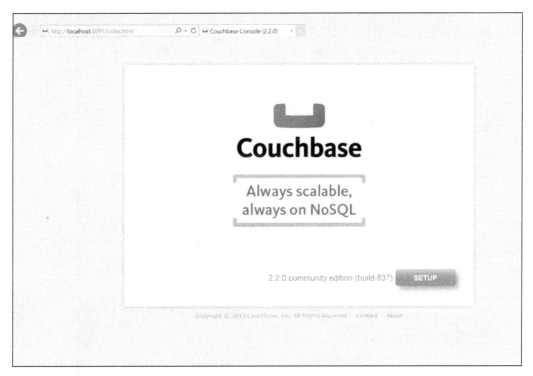

Couchbase Console for new install

The Couchbase Web Console provides a setup utility to get your cluster up and running. Click on the blue **Setup** button to begin. The following screenshot shows the configuration screen:

Configuring the server

The options found in step 1 of the configuration screen are fairly straightforward. The first two fields are the paths where Couchbase will store data and indexes. The server hostname uniquely identifies a node in a cluster. I'll discuss clusters in more detail later in this chapter. For now, you can think of a cluster as a collection of Couchbase server instances, or nodes, with the same buckets.

For development, it's generally useful to set this to 127.0.0.1. Basically, you want to ensure that whatever hostname you choose, it is not subject to change, as could be the case when running in the cloud or attaching the cluster to a network outside of your home or office.

The final option is whether to start a new cluster or connect to an existing cluster. In our case, we'll obviously be starting a new cluster. In a production environment, you'd want to maximize the amount of RAM available to your node. For development purposes, you are free to choose a lesser amount. The important thing to note here is that the amount of RAM you allocate will be required by each node in your cluster. If you click on the **Join a cluster now** option, you'll be asked to provide the address of a node in the cluster and the cluster credentials, as shown here:

○ Start a new cluster.

● Join a cluster now.

IP Address: 127.0.0.1

Username: Administrator

Password:

Connecting to a new cluster

Click on **Next** to be brought to step 2, where you'll be asked whether you want to install one of the two available sample buckets. We'll dig into buckets in the next step, so for now, just check the **beer-sample** bucket. That's the sample data source we'll use as we explore the development APIs. The following screen shows the sample buckets to be selected:

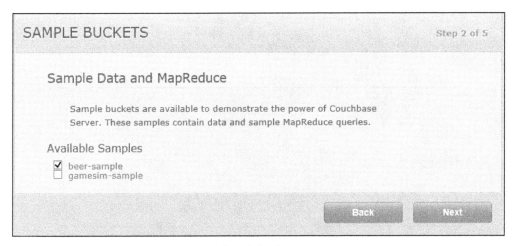

Sample buckets

In step 3, you're prompted to configure the default bucket for the new cluster. Couchbase buckets are loosely analogous to databases in relational systems. If you've used MySQL, SQL Server, or any other relational database server, you know that you must create an object called a database in which you'll create your tables and other database objects. Similarly, with Couchbase Server, a bucket is a container for the documents and indexes you'll store.

You must have at least one bucket on your cluster, and during the setup you are required to create a bucket named default. As you can see in the next screenshot, you are not allowed to change the name of this first bucket. You do, however, have other decisions to make about the default bucket.

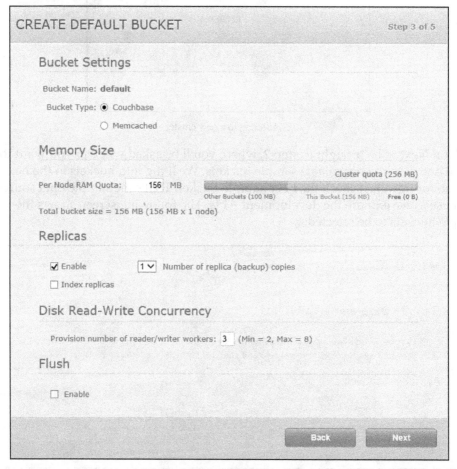

Bucket configuration

Couchbase, a being of Membase and therefore of Memcached lineage, fully supports the Memcached binary protocol. What this means is that Couchbase Server can be used as a stand-in replacement for a Memcached cluster. If you're currently using Memcached as a distributed cache for your application, you would be able to replace it with Couchbase Server and a Memcached bucket.

If you set the bucket type to Memcached, your bucket won't be persistent, and it won't be able to take advantage of the document capabilities that Couchbase provides. Even for use as a distributed cache, a Couchbase bucket is almost always the right choice. Couchbase disk writes are performed asynchronously, and it's unlikely that your application will be impeded by I/O problems. We'll stick to Couchbase buckets for this text, but it's important to understand the difference between these two bucket types.

Because Couchbase relies heavily on RAM to achieve its blazingly fast performance, it's important to allocate as much RAM as possible to your bucket. I'll discuss Couchbase Server's architecture towards the end of this chapter, but for now, know that more RAM generally means better performance. For development purposes, feel free to allocate the minimum amount of RAM required for each node (for instance, 100 MB).

Couchbase Server supports replication within your cluster. When you set up a bucket, you may choose to replicate the data to up to three other nodes. Replication will also be discussed at the end of this chapter. Since we are using a single-node cluster, uncheck the **Enable** option.

Couchbase allows you to specify the number of reader/writer workers to allocate for a bucket. This setting exists to allow administrators to optimize disk I/O. We'll leave the default value, 3, in place. If you enable **Flush** on your buckets, you'll have the ability to remove all documents from a bucket with a single command. This action is like truncating all the tables in your relational database, so obviously it should be set only when absolutely necessary.

In step 4, the wizard simply asks whether you wish to receive update notifications, and allows you to sign up for Couchbase's community update e-mails. Neither choice will affect the setup. The fifth and final step is to set up a username and password for cluster administration.

After completing the wizard, you'll be presented with a **Cluster Overview** page. When this page first loads, it's possible that you'll see a brief notification that the node is down while the bucket is activated. You're also likely to see a notification that the sample bucket is being loaded. Once ready, your cluster should show as healthy with active buckets, as in shown in the following screenshot:

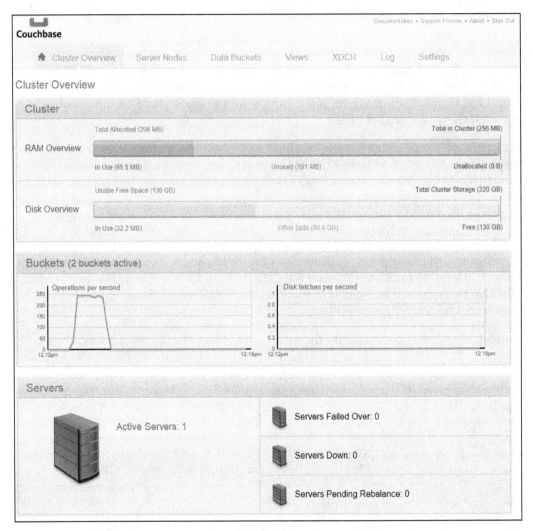

Initialization

Exploring the Couchbase Console

At this point, we'll take a quick tour of the other tabs found in the Couchbase Console, starting with the **Server Nodes** tab. When you click on this view first, you'll see a list of all active servers in your cluster. In our case, we have only one active server. For each of the nodes, you'll also see its status (**Up** or **Down**) and some vital stats such as RAM and CPU usage. Note that in the following screenshot, I clicked on the arrow next to the node name to reveal additional details about the node.

You'll also notice a button labeled **Pending Rebalance** next to the active servers. Nodes that appear in this list are those that are part of the cluster, but will not be fully active until they've been rebalanced. I'll discuss rebalancing at the end of this chapter. You'll also see options to trigger a rebalance and add another node to the cluster.

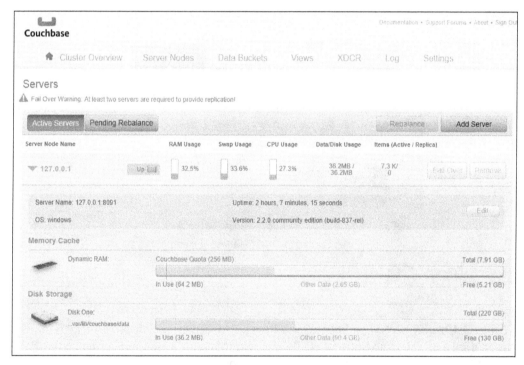

The Server Nodes tab

The **Data Buckets** tab lists all the buckets for a cluster. At this point, you should see both the **beer-sample** and **default** buckets. I expanded the **beer-sample** bucket in the following screenshot to reveal more detailed information about the bucket. You'll see options for viewing bucket documents and views. You may edit your existing buckets or create new buckets. You'll also see important stats such as item count and RAM and disk usage. We'll explore these options in more detail in the rest of the book.

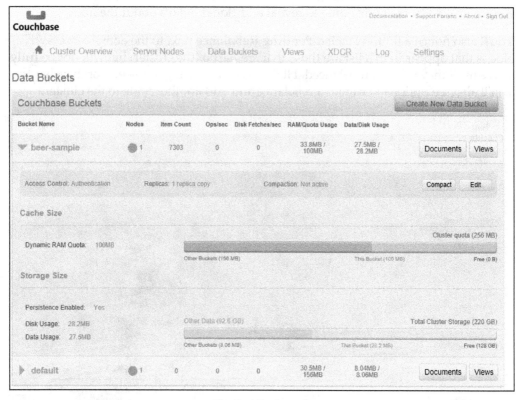

The Data Buckets tab

Chapter 3, Creating Secondary Indexes with Views, and *Chapter 4, Advanced Views*, will cover **Views** in detail, so for now we'll skip over this tab. Cross-data-center replication, or XDCR, allows you to create unidirectional or bidirectional replications of two clusters. XDCR is beyond the scope of this book, but know that you can manage it here. The **Log** tab shows the running server log. Some messages are only for information, while some expose failures on your server. On the **Settings** tab, you can perform a variety of tasks from adding a sample bucket to activating auto-failover.

Couchbase architecture

Before we move on to developing with Couchbase, it's useful to understand the general Couchbase architecture. While coding against a single-node cluster should generally be no different than coding against a 10-node cluster, supporting a production application does require deeper understanding of what could go wrong, as your application needs to scale out. In the following sections, I'll describe in more detail some of the concepts we've already seen, and the basics of how a Couchbase cluster operates.

Couchbase clusters

Fundamental to all Couchbase deployments is the notion of a **cluster**. This is a common term in the NoSQL world and generally refers to a collection of nodes performing operations on a data store in tandem. However, how nodes in a cluster behave varies significantly across NoSQL products. In some systems, all nodes are peers, with no differences. In others, clusters are set up in master-slave configurations.

In a Couchbase cluster, nodes are interchangeable. Each node contains a cluster manager, which is responsible for knowing the status of other nodes in the cluster, and for allowing other nodes to know its status. As each node has its own cluster manager component, this allows Couchbase Server to scale out linearly with no single point of failure.

Replication

One of the most important tasks of the cluster manager is to ensure that all of the data is available to clients. Couchbase Server replication works by making one node the master node for a given document, while up to three slave nodes maintain a replica of that document. In case the cluster manager detects a node failure, it is responsible for promoting replicas to the primary node.

Balancing and rebalancing

Sharding is the notion of distributing data evenly across the nodes of a cluster. In most sharded systems, the admin is responsible for picking a shard key to be used for data distribution. For example, a Users table might be sharded on a Username field. If the shard key turns out to be poorly distributed (imagine 30 percent of users having usernames starting with T), then the nodes will not be well balanced.

Couchbase, in contrast, is auto-sharded and guarantees balance. Recall that Couchbase documents are stored using a key/value approach. Though the user supplies the key, Couchbase SDKs use a strong and cryptographic hash on each key to guarantee that keys will be evenly distributed across a cluster. This hashing action considers the topology of the cluster, which means that whether there are 2 or 20 nodes, the keys will still be balanced.

Even though the SDKs and the server work together to ensure proper sharding, in case a node (or nodes) goes offline, that balance will temporarily be broken. This is because replicas are promoted. As nodes are added or removed from a cluster, the cluster manager will work to rebalance the data across the nodes. A newly added node may not be ready to fully join the cluster until a rebalance has been performed. As alluded to earlier, this task may be done using the Couchbase Console.

Couchbase SDKs

We'll explore the Couchbase SDK and relevant APIs in detail over the next few chapters. But to complete our discussion on balancing and rebalancing, it's useful to understand the process from client to cluster. When an SDK is initialized in a client application, it makes a persistent connection to the cluster over a RESTful API. This API broadcasts a JSON message containing the cluster's topology. As nodes are added or removed, the cluster sends a new message with an updated topology.

This behavior sets Couchbase apart from other databases, whether relational or nonrelational. Most database systems have a central point of communication that is responsible for client communications. Couchbase owes some of its massive throughput to its smart clients. Eliminating the bottleneck of a man-in-the-middle allows performance levels to reach a massive scale. On a cluster with only four nodes, Couchbase is capable of achieving nearly 1 million operations per second.

Returning to the idea of balancing data across nodes, there's an additional detail that I didn't mention. The cluster maintains an abstraction known as **vBuckets**, which are used to direct a key to the correct server. Rather than mapping a key directly to a node, Couchbase SDKs map the key to one of the vBuckets. The endpoint for a vBucket is provided to the client as part of its topology message from the cluster. Regardless of the number of nodes, the number of vBuckets remains the same. The keys always hash to the same vBucket, even if the cluster changes the endpoint of the vBucket.

While you'll generally not need to worry about the existence of vBuckets, it is important to understand what happens on the client as the cluster changes its topology. The client maintains a map of vBuckets to the nodes. If that map changes due to a node failure, brief client failures may appear while the map is updated.

> The only case where you're likely to care about vBuckets is if you are developing an application using Mac OS X. On this platform, Couchbase Server uses 64 vBuckets instead of the standard 1024. While this difference generally won't impact your development, it will impede your ability to move data from your local server to another cluster running Linux or Windows.

RAM matters

Couchbase is a "RAM first, disk second" database. Both the reads and writes are optimized to use RAM. On the write side, documents are written to the memory first and then flushed asynchronously to the disk. While volatile memory might not seem optimal for a database, remember that Couchbase will replicate your data on up to three nodes. Additionally, there are API methods that require a disk write before a write to RAM is considered a success.

On the read side, Couchbase maintains metadata about documents in the RAM to provide faster retrieval. Couchbase will also attempt to store as many documents as it is able to in the memory for faster access. Less available RAM means that Couchbase will need to fetch more documents from the disk. Couchbase uses a **most recently used (MRU)** algorithm to determine which documents are cached and which are evicted. The current beta version, Couchbase Server 3.0, will allow caching and eviction strategies to be tuned.

Summary

As we saw, Couchbase is an extremely flexible and scalable database. It offers a set of complimentary key/value and document features not found in any other database. In the next few chapters, we'll explore these features in detail. You will learn how and when to use them.

We also set up our single-node Couchbase cluster. Our default and sample buckets were created. We explored the Couchbase Console and discussed cluster architecture. With this knowledge in hand, you're ready to dig into application development with Couchbase.

If you've used either Memcached or CouchDB, you'll find the next three chapters to be somewhat familiar. In the next chapter, we're going to dig deep into Couchbase's key/value API. As we'll see, at first it will look a lot like Memcached, but it'll quickly go above and beyond.

2
Using Couchbase CRUD Operations

Couchbase Server has a vast and powerful key/value API. There are basic operations to read and write values. There are facilities for easy and quick modification of simple data types. There are also methods used to manage concurrency with locks. You'll even find advanced key/value API methods that allow you to verify persistence and replication. In this chapter, we're going to explore the key/value interface in detail.

In order to examine this API, you'll need to install one of the Couchbase SDKs. While the Couchbase Console provides tools to insert and update documents, it doesn't expose the Couchbase CRUD API to the user in any way. To get a full feel for the Couchbase key/value API, we're going to jump right into using an SDK.

The Couchbase SDKs

The Couchbase team supports a number of SDKs, also known as Couchbase client libraries. At the time of writing this book, there are official libraries for Java, .NET, PHP, Ruby, Python, C, and Node.js. There are also community-supported libraries for Perl, Erlang, Go, and other platforms.

In this chapter, we'll explore a few of these clients. You should install the library for the platform with which you are most comfortable. Many of the clients are available through package managers such as .NET's NuGet or Python's pip. Visit http://www.couchbase.com/communities to find instructions about installation. Each community has a *Getting Started* guide that details how to obtain your chosen SDK, as shown next:

Getting a client up and running in your environment of choice is beyond the scope of this chapter. If you wish to follow along with the examples, then you should run through the *Getting Started* tutorial for your platform. In the final chapter, we'll work through building a to-do list application, where we'll explore SDK usage in more detail. If you get stuck, be sure to check out the community forums.

Basic operations

Couchbase Server's key/value API includes standard CRUD operations, and each of the SDKs contains corresponding CRUD methods. We'll begin our API exploration by demonstrating how to insert and retrieve a record from our default bucket. If you're following along, make sure you read the *Getting Started* guide's description on how to configure your client for use.

Connecting to your cluster

Before reading from or writing to a Couchbase Server bucket, you must first configure your client. The basic setup is consistent across all SDKs. You first connect to the cluster and then open a connection to a bucket, as follows:

```
var cluster = new Cluster();
var bucket = cluster.OpenBucket();
```

In the preceding C# snippet, the client assumes that the cluster is located on localhost (127.0.0.1), and the bucket you're connecting to is default. You can also set these values explicitly, like this:

```
var cluster = new Cluster("127.0.0.1");
var bucket = cluster.OpenBucket("default");
```

If you have multiple nodes in your cluster, you can supply multiple nodes when creating the cluster. If your bucket has a password, you can also specify that when opening the bucket:

```
var cluster = new Cluster("192.168.0.1", "192.168.0.2");
var bucket = cluster.OpenBucket("beer-sample", "b33rs@mpl3");
```

It's also possible to manage your cluster using SDKs. For example, if you want to create a bucket programmatically in .NET, you can use the ClusterManager class and its management APIs:

```
var mgr = cluster.CreateManager("Administrator", "password");
mgr.CreateBucket("beer-sample");
```

Creating and updating a record

With any database system, create is the CRUD method with which you'll generally begin creating a record (assuming you have no data yet). There are a couple of different methods for creating a record in a Couchbase bucket, the simplest of which is add. The add method takes a key and a corresponding value. Then it inserts the pair into your bucket:

```
client.add("message", "Hello, Couchbase World!")
```

The preceding Python snippet demonstrates adding a record with a value of Hello, Couchbase World! and a message key. If no record with a message key existed when you ran this code, a record will be created. If you try to run the same code again, you'll receive an error. The add method fails when trying to write a value to an existing key.

If you want to update the message record, then you should use the replace method. This method performs an update to a document with an existing key. The following Python snippet demonstrates how to use this method:

```
client.replace("message", "Hello, Couchbase World!")
```

In the preceding example, the Hello, Couchbase World! value will be replaced with Hello, Couchbase SDK World!, leaving a document with a message key and a Hello, Couchbase World! value. Similar to add, the replace method will fail if you try to update a record using a key that does not exist.

You might be wondering how to work around these potential failures. Fortunately, Couchbase provides a third CRUD operation called set. The set operation behaves as a combination of both add and replace. If you try to set a record with a key that does not exist, set will perform an add operation. If you try to set a value for a key that does exist, set will perform a replace operation.

```
client.replace("message", "Hello, Couchbase World!")
```

You'll realize that using the set method is generally the easiest option. However, there will be occasions where using add or replace makes more sense. For example, using add instead of set would allow you to have keys based on a user's nickname without worrying about a collision wiping out an existing record.

For bulk operations, some SDKs support a multi_set operation. When using this method, you supply a dictionary structure instead of a single key and value. The keys and values from the dictionary are sent to the server and processed concurrently. The client SDKs will determine which node owns which keys and send them in parallel. The multi_set operation will almost always be faster than a single set operation:

```
messages = { "Alice" : "Hello!", "Bob" : "Cheers!" }
client.multi_set(messages)
```

The Python snippet we just saw demonstrates writing multiple keys to the server in a single call. At the time of writing this book, not all SDKs support multi_set, though support should be on the roadmaps of those that don't.

Reading and deleting records

Reading a value from the server is performed by providing a key for the Get command. If the key exists on the server, Get will return the value. If the key doesn't exist, then the SDK will return either its language's version of null (for example, None in Python or nil in Ruby) or a wrapper around the result, which is the case with .NET and Java:

```
var result = bucket.Get<string>("message");
```

The preceding C# snippet demonstrates retrieving a record from the server and assigning it to a local variable. In this case, the result variable will be of the IOperationResult<T> type. It will contain properties that indicate whether the operation succeeded as well as the value itself:

```
if (result.Success)
{
    Console.WriteLine(result.Value);
}
```

When using SDKs from one of the strongly-typed platforms (for example, .NET or Java), you'll likely want to cast the value to a specific type. The C# `Get` example we just saw sets the generic type parameter to a string and tells the client to treat the stored object as a .NET string.

It's important to know the type of data you've stored with a particular key. If you try to cast the result of a `Get` operation to the wrong data type, your SDK will likely raise a cast exception of some sort. In the .NET client, if you supply an incorrect generic type parameter, then `InvalidCastException` will be thrown:

```
var result = bucket.Get<int>("message");
```

The .NET client will catch the exception in this case. The caught exception is available in the `Exception` property of the `result` variable. The `Success` property will also be set to `false`, allowing you to react to the exception:

```
if (!result.Success&&result.Exception != null)
{
    Console.WriteLine(result.Exception.Message);
}
```

The `Value` property of the `result` variable will be zero (the default value for integers in .NET) after the assignment in the previous example completes. When a non-primitive type is supplied as the generic type parameter, `Value` would be null (the default for non-primitive types). As such, it is not sufficient to check if `Value` is null to know whether the key was found.

Because Couchbase Server does not explicitly define data types for your records, your SDK will decide what type it should serialize and deserialize values to. Cast and use type methods carefully to avoid errors in your application.

 You should be aware that a client may raise a "not found" error instead of null. However, this is a typical behavior, and you must explicitly enable it. Moreover, most SDKs don't expose this behavior. With the Python and Ruby clients, you are able to enable or disable "not found" exceptions by passing a `quiet` parameter to the `get` method.

There is also a variant of the `Get` operation that allows you to retrieve multiple values at once by providing multiple keys. When you use `Get` in this way, the SDKs will return a sort of dictionary structure where each of the keys in the dictionary will be the keys for which you requested values. The values of the dictionary will be the values from those keys on the server, or null if no values are found:

```
bucket.Insert("artist", "Arcade Fire");
bucket.Insert("album", "Funeral");
```

```
bucket.Insert("track", "Neighborhood #1 (Tunnels)");

var keys = new List<string> { "artist", "album", "track"};
var results = bucket.Get<string>(keys);

foreach (var key in keys)
{
    Console.WriteLine(results[key].Value);
}
```

The preceding C# snippet demonstrates how to read multiple keys at once and iterate over the resulting IDictionary object. The exact data structure returned by the SDK will, of course, vary according to the language you use, but it will be an iterable key/value structure.

The multi-get operation is implemented in the SDKs using parallel operations. More precisely, the client figures out which keys are on which servers, and then makes concurrent requests to each server. The client then returns the unified map object. This concurrency almost always means that it is more efficient to request many keys at once, as opposed to performing many individual Get operations serially.

To remove a key from the server, you'll simply pass that key to the delete operation on your SDK. Deleting a key using the .NET SDK is done as follows:

```
bucket.remove("message");
```

Advanced CRUD operations

The basic CRUD operations we've just seen are fairly straightforward and mimic what you'd expect to see in a relational system. As a key/value store, however, Couchbase provides a handful of additional, unique CRUD operations.

Temporary keys

As a descendant of the in-memory-only Memcached, Couchbase supports a set of operations you might not expect to see in a persistent store. Specifically, each of the CRUD methods outlined allows an expiry date to be provided. When set, this "time to live" option will be used to trigger the removal of a key by the server.

It is common in relational systems to have tables with expiration date columns. In this case, the expiry date is likely a flag to be used by a scheduled task that cleans old records. Couchbase Server allows you to achieve this very functionality without the need for a scheduled task or additional properties in the stored value.

To create a key with an expiry date, you can use either the `set` or `add` operation. You'll use these methods just as you used them previously, but you'll provide the additional "time to live" argument. In the following Python snippet, the key is set to expire in 1 hour:

```
client.set("message", "Goodbye, Couchbase World!", ttl = 3600)
```

How the expiry flag is set will vary by client, but it is commonly an integer value. In the case of .NET, it is set using .NET date and time structures.

You might wish to cause your keys to expire based on when they were last accessed. Using `touch` operations, you are able to achieve this sort of sliding expiry for your keys. The standard `Get` operation includes a time-to-live option. When you include a value for this parameter, you reset (or set) the time-to-live for the key:

```
client.get("message", ttl = 3600)
```

This Python snippet will reset the expiry on the `message` key to 1 hour from when the `Get` operation is performed. If you wish to extend the life of a key but not return its value there is a `touch` operation. Again, this operation is shown as follows in Python:

```
client.touch("message", ttl = 3600)
```

Appending and incrementing data

Couchbase Server also provides the ability to append or prepend additional data to (typically) string values. These operations are useful to store data structures such as delimited lists of values. Consider a key that stores tags for a blog post. One option would be to serialize and deserialize a list structure through your SDK:

```
tags = ["python", "couchbase", "nosql"]
client.set("tags", tags)
saved_tags = client.get("tags")
```

While this option would certainly work, it does require additional work to update data. You'd need to retrieve the record, update it in the memory, and then write it back to the server. Moreover, you'd also likely need to use a locking operation to ensure that the list hasn't changed since you retrieved it.

Another possibility is to use the `append` operation. With the `append` operation, you can push data to the end of a key's value. The concatenation takes place on the server, which means you don't have to manipulate the existing value first. The following Python snippet demonstrates the usage of `append`. In this example, we're maintaining the list of tags as a simple, comma-delimited string:

```
client.set("tags", "python,couchbase,")
client.append("tags", "nosql,")
saved_tags = client.get("tags")
#saved_tags == "python,couchbase,nosql,"
```

Similarly, Couchbase supports a `prepend` operation to save data to the beginning of a key's value, as seen next in the Python snippet:

```
client.set("tags", "python,couchbase,")
client.prepend("tags", "nosql,")
saved_tags = client.get("tags")
#saved_tags  == "couchbase,nosql,python,"
```

Another useful operation is increment. This command provides a means of updating an integer value on the server. Similar to `prepend` and `append`, `incr` allows you to modify a key's value without having to modifying it in your client application. Incrementing a counter is the most common use of this feature:

```
client.set("counter", 1)
client.incr("counter") # counter == 2
client.incr("counter", 4) # counter == 6
```

The preceding Python sample shows that the default increment behavior is to add 1 to the existing value of the key. If you provide a value for the offset parameter, the key's value will be incremented by the offset. If you want to decrement a counter, you can provide a negative offset value:

```
client.incr("counter", -1)
```

There is also a decrement operation, and it can be used instead of a negative offset with increment:

```
client.decr("counter", 1)
```

Storing complex types

So far, we've limited our exploration primarily to simple data types such as strings and integers. In a real application, you're more likely to have business objects or other complex types that you will need to store. To Couchbase Server, the values that you store are nothing more than byte arrays. Therefore, the SDKs are able to use their respective language's binary serializer (often called a **transcoder**) to store any data structures.

Consider an application that stores information on a user profile. In .NET, you might have a data object that looks like this:

```
public class UserProfile
{
  public string Username { get; set; }

  public string Email { get; set; }
}
```

When you use the .NET client to save an instance of the UserProfile class in Couchbase Server, it will be serialized using .NET's default binary serializer. Couchbase Server, of course, knows nothing about a client platform's serialization format. It will simply store the byte array it received from the client:

```
var userProfile = new UserProfile {
Username = "jsmith", Email = "js@asdf.com" };
client.Upsert(userProfile.Username, userProfile);
```

In the preceding snippet, an instance of the UserProfile class is saved with a key value that is set to the user's username. To retrieve that instance, simply use the Get operation we've already seen. This time, our SDK's transcoder will return an instance of UserProfile set as the value property of the result variable:

```
var result = client.Get<UserProfile>("jsmith");
```

Recall that if the value for the jsmith key is not an instance of UserProfile, the operation will fail with an invalid cast exception being thrown.

It is important to note that platform-specific serializers may not be compatible between SDKs. Imagine you have the following Python class (full class definition omitted for brevity):

```
class UserProfile:
  @property
  def username(self):
    pass
```

```
@property
def email(self):
    pass
```

If you tried to retrieve the .NET-serialized `UserProfile` object and deserialize it into an instance of the preceding Python class, you'd encounter an exception. Python and .NET have different binary serialization formats:

```
client.get("jsmith") #will likely break
```

There is a solution to the problem of hybrid systems where multiple clients need to access Couchbase Server data from multiple frameworks. We'll explore that solution when we start to work with Couchbase Server's document-oriented features. For now, we'll assume that we're using a single-client SDK environment.

It's also worth noting that Couchbase SDKs support custom transcoders. If you want to change the default serialization behavior for your SDK, implementing your own transcoder is the way to achieve this goal. For example, if you want to force all of the data to be stored as JSON, a custom transcoder can solve this problem. You can also use the `data_passthrough` parameter in certain SDKs, which will force all values to be returned as raw bytes.

Concurrency and locking

While the Couchbase SDKs have been written to be thread-safe, your Couchbase applications still must consider concurrency. Whether two users or two threads are attempting to modify the same key, locking is a necessity in order to limit stale data writes. Couchbase Server supports both pessimistic and optimistic locking.

The CRUD operations we've seen so far do not make use of any locking. To see why this is a problem, consider the following C# code:

```
public class Story
{
public String Title { get; set; }
  public String Body { get; set; }
  public List<String> Comments { get; set; }
}

var story = bucket.Get<Story>("story_slug").Value;
story.Comments.add("Nice Article!");
bucket.Replace<Story>("story_slug", story);
```

Now suppose that in the preceding code, in the moments between the `get` and `set` calls, the following code ran on another thread (that is, another web request):

```
var story = bucket.get<Story>("story_slug");
story.Comments.add("Great writing!");
client.Replace<Story>("story_slug", story);
```

In this scenario, both clients received the same initial `Story` values. After the second client sets its value back in the bucket with a new comment, it is quickly overwritten because the first client completes its set. The `Great writing!` comment is lost. Fortunately, the Couchbase API does provide a mechanism to prevent this situation from occurring.

In traditional relational applications, a common pattern is to include a timestamp column on tables where stale records should not be updated without first retrieving the most recent write of a row. When this approach is used, the UPDATE statement includes the timestamp in the WHERE clause:

```
UPDATE Story
SET Title = 'New Title',
        Timestamp = @NewTimeStamp
WHERE ID = 1 AND Timestamp = @CurrentTimestamp;
```

In the preceding SQL statement, the update will not occur unless the row's current timestamp value is provided for the `@CurrentTimestamp` parameter. With Couchbase Server, you are able to use **CAS** (short for **compare and swap**) operations to provide the same optimistic locking.

CAS operations take advantage of the fact that with each mutation of a key, the server will maintain with it a unique 64-bit integer, known as a CAS. CAS operations work by disallowing a key's mutation if the provided CAS value doesn't match the server's current version. You could think of CAS as acting like a version control system. If you try to commit a patch without first getting the latest revisions, your commit fails. However, Couchbase does not maintain revisions for each CAS, it simply prevents stale writes:

```
var result = bucket.Get<Story>("story_slug");
var story = result.Value;
story.Comments.add("Awesome!");
var resp = bucket.Replace<Story>(result.Cas, "story_slug", story);
```

In the preceding C# example, the `result` variable is returned from the client by way of its `Get` method. This object contains both the stored object and the current CAS value from the server. That CAS value is used with a call to the `Replace` method. After the `Get` method is called, if another thread has updated the `story_slug` key, then the `Replace` call will not result in a mutated value. The response from the attempt will include the status of the operation:

```
if (resp.Success)
{
   //operation success
}
else if (resp.Status == ResponseStatus.KeyNotFound) {
   //key does not exist, use add instead
}
else if (resp.Status == ResponseStatus.KeyExists)
{
   //key exists, but CAS didn't match
   //call Getagain, try again
}
```

In this example, you can see that the C# client provides the three possible outcomes for a CAS operation. If the CAS is the same, the mutation occurs. If the key is not found, an insert operation should be performed. If the CAS is different, the mutation is stopped. The question that follows then is, how do you handle a CAS mismatch?

In the simplest case, you'd simply retry your `Get` and `Replace` operations, hoping that the CAS value you've obtained is now current. However, a more robust solution is to employ some sort of retry loop:

```
for(var i=0; i< 5; i++) {
   var result = bucket.Get<Story>("story_slug");
   var story = result.Value();
   story.Comments.add("Awesome!");
   var resp = bucket.Replace<Story>(result.Cas, "story_slug", story);

   if (resp.Success) break;
}
```

The advantage of this sort of locking is that it is optimistic, meaning that the server doesn't employ any locking of its own. One 64-bit integer is compared to another. If they match, the values for a key are swapped. This operation has virtually no impact on performance. However, it does make room for the possibility that a thread may never acquire a current CAS. If such a situation is unacceptable, Couchbase Server provides a pessimistic locking option.

The getl (or get and lock) operation allows you to obtain a read/write lock on a key for up to 30 seconds. While you hold the lock, no other clients or threads will be able to modify the key. You consume getl in a manner similar to the CAS operations. When you request a lock, you're provided a CAS with which only your client will be able to update the key:

```
var result= bucket.GetWithLock<Story>("story_slug", TimeSpan.
FromSeconds(10));
var story = result.Value;
story.Comments.Add("Good stuff!");
bucket.Replace<Story>("story_slug", story, result.Cas);
```

The preceding C# code demonstrates how a client may acquire an exclusive lock on a key. In this case, the lock will expire in 30 seconds. Clients who attempt to read or write to this key will receive an error. In this example, the lock will be released once the CAS operation is performed.

Rather than waiting for an expiry or a CAS operation, it is also possible to explicitly unlock a key. Generally speaking, a CAS operation is likely to be your primary means of unlocking a key. However, there will be times when some condition in your code leads to a path where the locked document shouldn't be mutated. In those cases, it's more efficient to unlock the document rather than wait for the timeout:

```
Var result  = bucket.GetWithLock<Story>("story_slug", TimeSpan.
FromSeconds(10))
if (result.value.IsCommentingClosed)
{
  bucket.Unlock("story_slug", result.Cas);
}
else
{
  result.value.Comments.Add("Couchbase is fast!");
  bucket.Replace<Story>("story_slug", story);
}
```

This C# code demonstrates retrieving a key, checking whether the value should be modified, and then deciding how to perform. In this example, we're checking whether commenting is closed for a story. If it is, we won't accept a new comment. Therefore, we'll release the lock rather than wait for the remaining 10 seconds.

When deciding between a CAS operation and a getl operation, you will have to consider whether you want other threads to be blocked from reading the locked key. In such a case, a GetWithLock method is required. More often, a CAS operation is probably the safest in terms of performance and side effects.

Asynchronous operations

One of the primary reasons for the growth of Couchbase is its massive scalability. Few databases come close to the performance offered by Couchbase Server. Any system that is capable of handling millions of operations per second across a small cluster of nodes will have to deal with concurrency issues at some point.

Traditionally, servers dealt with concurrency by spinning up threads to handle multiple requests simultaneously. However, as load increases on such systems, the overhead of creating and maintaining threads becomes quite expensive in terms of CPU and memory.

Couchbase Server makes use of nonblocking I/O libraries to provide scaling, without the need to spin a thread or process every request. In a nutshell, nonblocking I/O makes heavy use of asynchronous callbacks to avoid blocking the receiving thread.

In other words, the thread that receives the request will only delegate the work to be done, and later receive a notification when that work is done. This pattern of handling concurrency is popular in modern servers and frameworks, including Node.js and the **nginx** web server.

All the operations covered used so far are blocking. In other words, when your client calls Couchbase Server with a command, it blocks the calling thread until that operation completes. It is common to use Couchbase in a fire-and-forget fashion, and blocking calls slows this process down.

Some (but not all) clients support asynchronous operations. Clients such as Ruby and Node.js are built on top of the C library, which is fully asynchronous. Therefore, such libraries are able to piggyback on client implementation. The fully managed Java library does support asynchronous operations using **Java Futures**.

We won't explore the asynchronous operations in detail, as they are effectively similar to the operations we've already seen. The following Ruby snippet gives you a taste of how you'd use such a method:

```
client.run do |c|
c.get("message") {|ret| puts ret.value}
end
```

In this example, the client runs the get operation asynchronously. When the method returns, the callback (in curly braces) is executed. The thread that called client.run was not blocked while waiting on the get call. Similarly, in Java, you may use the asynchronous versions of operations to allow nonblocking calls to Couchbase Server:

```
String message;
GetFuture<Object> future = client.asyncGet("message");
message = (String)future.get(10, TimeUnit.SECONDS);
```

In this Java example, the client asynchronously retrieves the `message` key. The value of that key is then assigned back to the message variable with a wait timeout of 10 seconds. A try/catch block should wrap the `future.get` call, but was omitted for brevity.

Durability operations

In *Chapter 1*, *Getting Comfortable with Couchbase*, you learned that Couchbase Server handles reads and writes by writing to the memory first, and then writing asynchronously to the disk. The standard CRUD operations we've seen so far make no distinction between a key being written to the cluster memory and a key persisting in the disk.

If you've set up replication, you've likely guarded your data against potential data loss from a single server failing before flushing the key to the disk. However, there will be times when your business process cannot tolerate the possibility that a record did not persist. If you have such a requirement, Couchbase Server supports inclusion of durability requirements with your store requests.

These durability requirements are tunable to your specific needs. For example, you might wish to know whether a key was written to the disk on its master node and replicated to at least two nodes in the memory. To use a durability check with a .NET client, you will use the standard store method with additional arguments, as follows:

```
bucket.Upsert<string>("key", "value", PersistTo.One,
ReplicateTo.Two);
```

The `PersistTo` argument specifies that the operation must return a failure if the key hasn't persisted in the master node after a timeout (globally configurable). The `ReplicateTo` option adds the additional requirement that the key must be copied to least two nodes in the memory.

If your durability concern is only that the key is replicated, you can use the previous operation without the `PersistTo` argument. Similarly, you can check for persistence only by omitting the replication argument. Importantly, if any persistence option is set, success will occur only if the master node wrote the key to the disk. If the replica wrote a key to the disk somehow but the master died before it could do so, the store operation will fail.

It might seem counterintuitive, but it is also possible to use durability requirements with delete methods. Similar to writes, delete operations are also applied to the memory first. Therefore, if you want to be sure that a key was also removed from the disk, you should include a persistence requirement.

```
bucket.Remove("key", PersistTo.One);
```

The SDKs generally reuse their persistence enumerations in both store and delete operations. In the case of delete, `PersistTo` is perhaps more accurately thought of as `RemoveFrom`.

It is important to use durability requirements with care if your application is in need of the peak scale. With much of Couchbase Server's performance being dependent on its heavy use of cache, blocking disk writes will obviously introduce latency. Generally speaking, it's best to use durability requirements only when absolutely necessary. It is more important to enable replication in your cluster.

Summary

In this chapter, we explored the Couchbase Server key/value API in detail. You saw that Couchbase supports the basic CRUD operations you'd expect of a database system, whether relational or nonrelational. We examined operations that are unique to Couchbase, for example, `append` and `prepend` operations can be used to store data, while increment and decrement operations can be used to modify a key's value.

You learned how Couchbase supports both pessimistic and optimistic locking as well as basic strategies to use both. We explored the ability to use durability checks and asynchronous methods to tweak the performance of our application. Most importantly, we got a taste of a few of the client SDKs and how they perform the various operations.

At this point, we've explored about 98 percent of the Couchbase key/value API. There are a few other legacy methods that you might encounter, depending on your SDK; for example, the `flush` operation is used to remove all records from a bucket. The key/value version of this method has been deprecated in favor of the cluster API version, which is performed over HTTP. However, you might find this method still accessible, given the backward compatibility with Memcached.

Though we omitted 2 percent of the available key/value operations in this chapter, 98 percent of the methods we looked at should cover 100 percent of your key/value requirements. Moreover, the design of your application may reveal that the basic CRUD operations and CAS are sufficient to meet your requirements.

In the next chapter, we're going to start exploring the document capabilities of Couchbase Server. As we do, you'll learn how it complements the key/value API you just learned about.

3
Creating Secondary Indexes with Views

Now that we've examined Couchbase Server's key/value API, it's time to shift gears and look at its document-oriented features.

Couchbase documents

Documents in Couchbase are simply key/value pairs where the value is stored as a valid JSON document. The key/value API we learnt in *Chapter 2, Using Couchbase CRUD Operations*, is the same API we'll use to create JSON documents in the server. Generally, you'll use the client SDKs in combination with your platform's preferred JSON serializer, as shown in this C# snippet:

```
var user = new User { Name = "John" };
var json = JsonConvert.SerializeObject(user);
bucket.Upsert("jsmith", json);
```

In this example, the popular .NET JSON serializer is used to transform an instance of a .NET class into a valid JSON string. That string is then stored on Couchbase Server using the key/value set operation.

Similarly, to retrieve a JSON document from the server, you'll also use the key/value Get operation:

```
var json = bucket.Get<string>("jsmith");
var user = JsonConvert.DeserializeObject<User>(json);
```

In the case of retrieving a document, you'll typically retrieve the JSON string and allow your platform's JSON serializer to deserialize the JSON document into a strongly-typed object, which is a User instance in this example.

Of course, you are free to do whatever you wish with the JSON you retrieve. The Couchbase SDKs intentionally provide you with the freedom to choose your own JSON-to-object behavior. Rather than deserializing into a user-defined type as you just did, you might want to convert your JSON document into a dictionary. You also could choose to simply return the JSON document to your application. This last approach could be particularly useful when serving JSON to JavaScript-heavy applications.

Of course, being able to store JSON strings alone is not enough for a database to be considered document-oriented. For that classification, a data store must support some other document capabilities, most importantly document indexing and querying.

Couchbase indexes

We've already seen how Couchbase handles primary indexes for documents. The key in the key/value pair is the unique primary key for a document. Using the key/value API, documents may be retrieved only by this key. While this might seem limiting, there are key/value schema design patterns that help to provide flexibility. We'll explore them in *Chapter 5, Introducing N1QL*.

Fortunately, Couchbase as a document store provides a much more powerful approach for finding your documents. To illustrate the problem and the solution, we'll walk through a brief example. Imagine having a simple JSON document such as this:

```
{
    "Username": "jsmith",
    "Email": "jsmith@somedomain.com"
}
```

The key/value limitation is easy to see. Imagine we want to find a user by their username. The key/value solution might be to use the username as the key. While that would certainly work, what happens when we also want to query a user by their e-mail address? We can't have both e-mail and username as a key!

Therefore, there are key/value patterns to address this problem, and we'll discuss them briefly later on. Couchbase, with its document capabilities, provides a much more elegant solution—allowing arbitrary secondary indexes on stored JSON documents.

These secondary indexes will allow us to query our user document by username, e-mail, or any function of the two (for example, an e-mail ID with a particular domain). These indexes, which are known as views in Couchbase terms, will be created using JavaScript and **MapReduce**.

MapReduce

Before we can start our exploration of the Couchbase Server views, we first need to understand what MapReduce is and how we'll use it to create secondary indexes for our documents.

At its simplest, MapReduce is a programming pattern used to process large amounts of data that is typically distributed across several nodes in parallel. In the NoSQL world, MapReduce implementations may be found on many platforms from MongoDB to Hadoop, and of course Couchbase.

Even if you're new to the NoSQL landscape, it's quite possible that you've already worked with a form of MapReduce. The inspiration for MapReduce in distributed NoSQL systems was drawn from the functional programming concepts of map and reduce. While purely functional programming languages haven't quite reached mainstream status, languages such as Python, C#, and JavaScript all support map and reduce operations.

Map functions

Consider the following Python snippet:

```
numbers = [1, 2, 3, 4, 5]
doubled = map(lambda n: n * 2, numbers)
#doubled == [2, 4, 6, 8, 10]
```

These two lines of code demonstrate a very simple use of a `map()` function. In the first line, the `numbers` variable is created as a list of integers. The second line applies a function to the list to create a new mapped list. In this case, the `map()` function is supplied as a Python `lambda`, which is just an inline, unnamed function. The body of `lambda` multiplies each number by two.

This `map()` function can be made slightly more complex by doubling only odd numbers, as shown in this code:

```
numbers = [1, 2, 3, 4, 5]
defdouble_odd(num):
  if num % 2 == 0:
    return num
  else:
    return num * 2

doubled = map(double_odd, numbers)
#doubled == [2, 2, 6, 4, 10]
```

Map functions are implemented differently in each language or platform that supports them, but all follow the same pattern. An iterable collection of objects is passed to a map function. Each item of the collection is then iterated over, with the map function being applied to that iteration. The final result is a new collection where each of the original items is transformed by the map.

Reduce functions

Like maps, reduce functions also work by applying a provided function to an iterable data structure. The key difference between the two is that the reduce function works to produce a single value from the input iterable. Using Python's built-in `reduce()` function, we can see how to produce a sum of integers, as follows:

```
numbers = [1, 2, 3, 4, 5]
sum = reduce(lambda x, y: x + y, numbers)
#sum == 15
```

You probably noticed that unlike our map operation, the reduce `lambda` has two parameters (x and y in this case). The argument passed to x will be the accumulated value of all applications of the function so far, and y will receive the next value to be added to the accumulation.

Parenthetically, the order of operations can be seen as $((((1 + 2) + 3) + 4) + 5)$. Alternatively, the steps are shown in the following list:

1. x = 1, y = 2
2. x = 3, y = 3
3. x = 6, y = 4
4. x = 10, y = 5
5. x = 15

As this list demonstrates, the value of x is the cumulative sum of previous x and y values. As such, reduce functions are sometimes termed **accumulate** or **fold** functions. Regardless of their name, reduce functions serve the common purpose of combining pieces of a recursive data structure to produce a single value.

Couchbase MapReduce

Creating an index (or view) in Couchbase requires creating a map function written in JavaScript. When the view is created for the first time, the map function is applied to each document in the bucket containing the view. When you update a view, only new or modified documents are indexed. This behavior is known as **incremental MapReduce**.

You can think of a basic map function in Couchbase as being similar to a SQL CREATE INDEX statement. Effectively, you are defining a column or a set of columns, to be indexed by the server. Of course these are not columns, but rather properties of the documents to be indexed.

Basic mapping

To illustrate the process of creating a view, first imagine that we have a set of JSON documents as shown here:

```
var books=[
    {
"id": 1,
"title": "The Bourne Identity",
"author": "Robert Ludlow"
    },
    {
"id": 2,
"title": "The Godfather",
"author": "Mario Puzzo"
    },
    {
"id": 3,
"title": "Wiseguy",
"author": "Nicholas Pileggi"
    }
];
```

Each document contains title and author properties. In Couchbase, to query these documents by either title or author, we'd first need to write a map function. Without considering how map functions are written in Couchbase, we're able to understand the process with vanilla JavaScript:

```
books.map(function(book) {
   return book.author;
});
```

In the preceding snippet, we're making use of the built-in JavaScript array's map() function. Similar to the Python snippets we saw earlier, JavaScript's map() function takes a function as a parameter and returns a new array with mapped objects. In this case, we'll have an array with each book's author, as follows:

```
["Robert Ludlow", "Mario Puzzo", "Nicholas Pileggi"]
```

At this point, we have a mapped collection that will be the basis for our author index. However, we haven't provided a means for the index to be able to refer back to the original document. If we were using a relational database, we'd have effectively created an index on the `Title` column with no way to get back to the row that contained it.

With a slight modification to our map function, we are able to provide the key (the `id` property) of the document as well in our index:

```
books.map(function(book) {
  return [book.author, book.id];
});
```

In this slightly modified version, we're including the ID with the output of each `author`. In this way, the index has its document's key stored with its title.

```
[["The Bourne Identity", 1], ["The Godfather", 2], ["Wiseguy", 3]]
```

We'll soon see how this structure more closely resembles the values stored in a Couchbase index.

Basic reducing

Not every Couchbase index requires a reduce component. In fact, we'll see that Couchbase already comes with built-in reduce functions that will provide you with most of the reduce behavior you need. However, before relying on only those functions, it's important to understand why you'd use a reduce function in the first place.

Returning to the preceding example of the map, let's imagine we have a few more documents in our set, as follows:

```
var books=[
    {
"id": 1,
"title": "The Bourne Identity",
"author": "Robert Ludlow"
    },
    {
"id": 2,
"title": "The Bourne Ultimatum",
"author": "Robert Ludlow"
    },
    {
"id": 3,
```

```
"title": "The Godfather",
"author": "Mario Puzzo"
        },
        {
"id": 4,
"title": "The Bourne Supremacy",
"author": "Robert Ludlow"
        },
        {
"id": 5,
"title": "The Family",
"author": "Mario Puzzo"
        },
   {
"id": 6,
"title": "Wiseguy",
"author": "Nicholas Pileggi"
        }
    ];
```

We'll still create our index using the same map function because it provides a way of accessing a book by its author. Now imagine that we want to know how many books an author has written, or (assuming we had more data) the average number of pages written by an author.

These questions are not possible to answer with a map function alone. Each application of the map function knows nothing about the previous application. In other words, there is no way for you to compare or accumulate information about one author's book to another book by the same author.

Fortunately, there is a solution to this problem. As you've probably guessed, it's the use of a reduce function. As a somewhat contrived example, consider this JavaScript:

```
mapped = books.map(function (book) {
    return ([book.id, book.author]);
});

counts = {}
reduced = mapped.reduce(function(prev, cur, idx, arr) {
var key = cur[1];
    if (! counts[key]) counts[key] = 0;
    ++counts[key]
}, null);
```

This code doesn't quite reflect the way you would count books with Couchbase accurately, but it illustrates the basic idea. You look for each occurrence of a key (author) and increment a counter when it is found. With Couchbase MapReduce, the mapped structure is supplied to the reduce() function in a better format. You won't need to keep track of items in a dictionary.

Couchbase views

At this point, you should have a general sense of what MapReduce is, where it came from, and how it will affect the creation of a Couchbase Server view. So without further ado, let's see how to write our first Couchbase view.

In *Chapter 1, Getting Comfortable with Couchbase*, we saw that when we install Couchbase Server, we have the option of including a sample bucket. In fact, there were two to choose from. The bucket we'll use is **beer-sample**. If you didn't install it, don't worry. You can add it by opening the Couchbase Console and navigating to the **Settings** tab. Here, you'll find the option to install the bucket, as shown next:

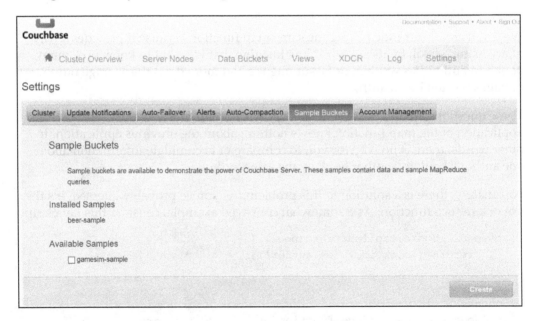

In the next sections, we'll return to the console to create our view, examine documents, and query our views. For now, however, we'll simply examine the code. First, you need to understand the document structures with which you're working. The following JSON object is a beer document (abbreviated for brevity):

```
{
  "name": "Sundog",
  "type": "beer",
  "brewery_id": "new_holland_brewing_company",
  "description": "Sundog is an amber ale...",
  "style": "American-Style Amber/Red Ale",
  "category": "North American Ale"
}
```

As you can see, the beer documents have several properties. We're going to create an index to let us query these documents by name. In SQL, the query would look like this:

```
SELECT Id FROM Beers WHERE Name = ?
```

You might be wondering why the SQL example includes only the Id column in its projection. We'll explore this analogy when we discuss view queries later in this chapter. For now, just know that to query a document using a view with Couchbase, the property by which you're querying must be included in an index.

To create that index, we'll write a map function. The simplest example of a map function to query beer documents by name is as follows:

```
function(doc) {
    emit(doc.name);
}
```

This body of the map function has only one line. It calls the built-in Couchbase emit() function. This function is used to signal that a value should be indexed. The output of this map function will be an array of names.

The **beer-sample** bucket includes brewery data as well. These documents look like the following code (abbreviated for brevity):

```
{
    "name": "Thomas Hooker Brewing",
    "city": "Bloomfield",
    "state": "Connecticut",
    "website": "http://www.hookerbeer.com/",
    "type": "brewery"
}
```

If we reexamine our map function, we'll see an obvious problem, both the brewery and beer documents have a `name` property. When this map function is applied to the documents in the bucket, it will create an index with documents from either the brewery or beer documents.

The problem is that Couchbase documents exist in a single container — the bucket. There is no namespace for a set of related documents. The solution has typically involved including a `type` or `docType` property on each document. The value of this property is used to distinguish one document from another.

In the case of the `beer-sample` database, beer documents have `type = "beer"` and brewery documents have `type = "brewery"`. Therefore, we are easily able to modify our map function to create an index only on beer documents:

```
function(doc) {
  if (doc.type == "beer") {
    emit(doc.name);
  }
}
```

The `emit()` function actually takes two arguments. The first, as we've seen, emits a value to be indexed. The second argument is an optional value and is used by the reduce function. Imagine that we want to count the number of beer types in a particular category. In SQL, we would write the following query:

```
SELECT Category, COUNT(*) FROM Beers GROUP BY Category
```

To achieve the same functionality with Couchbase Server, we'll need to use both map and reduce functions. First, let's write the map. It will create an index on the `category` property:

```
function(doc) {
  if (doc.type == "beer") {
    emit(doc.category, 1);
  }
}
```

The only real difference between our `category` index and our `name` index is that we're including an argument for the `value` parameter of the `emit()` function. What we'll do with that value is simply count them. This counting will be done in our reduce function:

```
function(keys, values) {
  return values.length;
}
```

In this example, the `values` parameter will be given to the reduce function as a list of all values associated with a particular key. In our case, for each beer category there will be a list of ones (that is, `[1, 1, 1, 1, 1, 1]`). Couchbase also provides a built-in `_count` function. It can be used in place of the entire reduce function in the preceding example.

Now that we've seen the basic requirements when creating an actual Couchbase view, it's time to add a view to our bucket. The easiest way to do so is to use the Couchbase Console.

Couchbase Console

In *Chapter 1, Getting Comfortable with Couchbase,* we skipped the **Views** tab in the Couchbase Web Console with the promise of returning to it in later chapters. It's just about time to fulfill that promise, but first we'll take a look at another tab we skipped — the **Data Buckets** tab.

Open Couchbase Console. As a reminder, it's found at `http://localhost:8091`. If you're using Couchbase on a server other than your laptop, substitute that server's name for `localhost`. After logging in, navigate to the **Data Buckets** tab, as shown here:

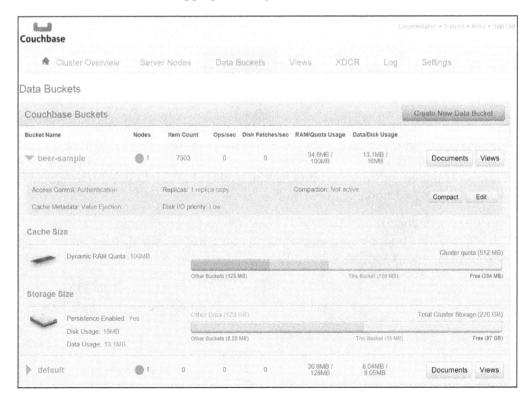

The **Data Buckets** tab provides you with a high-level overview of your buckets. You'll see each bucket listed with information ranging from server resource utilization to item (document) count. Feel free to explore some of the other features of this tab. This is where you are able to create and edit buckets. What we're most interested in is checking out the documents in our bucket. Click on the **Documents** button in the **beer-sample** bucket row, as shown next:

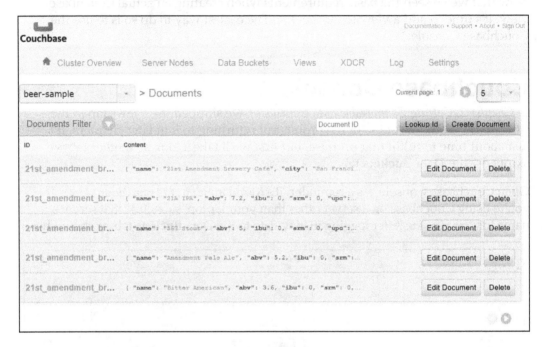

On this screen, you'll be able to browse for a document by its key or simply go through all the documents in the bucket. Select the **beer-sample** bucket from the drop-down menu above the list of documents. You'll then be able to browse through the sample beer and brewery documents. You're also able to edit or add documents to a bucket using additional features on this tab.

On a side note, if you followed along with an SDK in *Chapter 2, Using Couchbase CRUD Operations*, and looked up one of the documents you saved, you'd have noticed that you don't see JSON, but rather something that looks like what is shown in the following screenshot:

Earlier in this chapter, we learned that Couchbase Server recognizes proper JSON strings and treats them differently. Any value you store that is not JSON is treated by Couchbase Server as a byte array. Its meaning is up to your application to define. When you view a non-JSON-valued key in the document view, you'll be shown a base64 representation of that key's value.

While these documents are technically accessible to views, practically speaking you're highly unlikely to ever use a non-JSON record in your views. You could decode a base64 value in JavaScript, but we'll work with the assumption that you don't want to do so.

A common problem new Couchbase developers encounter is that they didn't provide proper JSON to the server, and they are unable to retrieve expected documents when querying a view. Checking for a base64-encoded string in the **Documents** page is a good way to eliminate bad JSON.

We're now ready to explore the **Views** tab, as shown here:

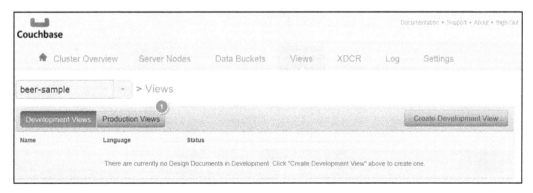

Development views

If you have a bucket with millions of documents, you probably won't want to trigger index creation with every tweak of your view definition during development. To allow developers to build views iteratively and quickly, Couchbase Server includes development views.

Unlike production views, development views are applied only to a subset of data from the bucket. Therefore, you are safely able to test a view definition against your production systems. Your application won't accidentally query one of these views either, because you must explicitly turn development views on for your chosen SDK.

After you've developed and tested your development view, you are able to promote it to production. At that time, the full bucket is indexed. In the Couchbase Console, you're able to edit only development views. Your production views are read-only.

The Couchbase REST admin API does allow you to work around this safety check by creating a view outside the confines of the console. You might choose to manage your views this way because it allows you to work more easily with source control or server automation tools.

We'll focus only on the Couchbase Console to create our views. To get started, click on the **Create Development View** button. You're then taken to a page where, at the top, there are dropdowns with your buckets and views in those buckets. Select the **beer-sample** bucket. This sample bucket includes three predefined views, as shown next. We'll create our own view rather than examining these.

Design documents

With the **beer-sample** bucket selected, click on the **Create Development View** button (ensure that **Development Views** is selected). In addition to providing a view name, you'll be prompted to provide a design document name, as shown here:

Naming a Development View

Views are defined in special documents on the server, known as a design documents. These documents are named with a prefix of _design/ followed by any meaningful name you choose. Additionally, development design documents will be named with a dev_ prefix.

Your design document may contain one or more view definitions. Typically, you're likely to have one design document for each document type (for example, one beer design document and one brewery document). However, our sample design document contains views for both breweries and beers.

 While adhering to the convention of one design document per document type is a good place to start, there are other factors that you must consider. Specifically, when you make any change to a design document, it triggers a re-indexing of all views defined within that design document. Therefore, it's best to segment views based on the likelihood of one document being updated.

Creating a view

Now that we know what design documents are, we're ready to create our first view. In the dialog box that appeared when you clicked on **Create Development View**, name the design document _design/dev_beers.

A useful convention for naming views is to prefix them with by_ and complete the name with the indexed fields. So, for the new view we're about to create (which indexes beer documents by their name property), set the name of the view to by_name.

After you've provided the design document name and view name, you'll see your view listed on the page. To edit this view, you could click on either the **Edit** button or the name of the view. Then you'll be presented with a simple editor in which you'll create your views, as shown next:

The default view that appears includes a map function. This map function looks slightly different from those we previously walked through. While it's mostly the same map function, notice the additional meta parameter. This optional parameter provides you with a way to access document metadata in your map function. Each document in Couchbase has a few fields of associated metadata. You can see these fields in the panel above the code editor (under **Preview a Random Document**).

More often than not, the only metadata field your views will be concerned with is the id field. This field is the key from the key/value API that is associated with a document. It's important to understand that the key is not part of the document, but rather a means of storing and retrieving the document.

The window that you see by default when you create a new view creates an index on document keys using the `meta` argument's `id` property. It might seem redundant to create a secondary index on the primary index. However, should you wish to perform range queries (that is, find all keys from *A* to *C*), then you'll need this index.

To create our view, we'll reuse the map function we wrote earlier in this chapter:

```
function(doc, meta) {
  if (doc.type == "beer") {
    emit(doc.name, null);
  }
}
```

After you've modified the map function to use this code, click on **Save** to start the process of indexing the documents. Once the map function is saved, we are able to test our view by clicking on the **Show Results** button under the code editor, as shown here:

The result you'll see is simply a list of every document that was included in the index. The `key` parameter in the index is the document's `name` property, ordered using Unicode collation. The value is `null` in this case because we did not include a second argument to our call to `emit()`. Notice that the document's `id` property is included under each of the index keys.

In many programming languages, sorting tends to follow byte order. If you sort a set of strings, most default implementations would follow ASCII ordering, which orders uppercase letters before lowercase variants. By contrast, Unicode collation orders variants of the same letter next to each other, as we have already discussed in a previous section.

 If you're unfamiliar with Unicode collation, you can think of it as being "not quite alphabetical." Though A will always be ordered before B, so will À. In other words, variations of letters will be ordered together before the next letter and its variations. Additionally, lowercase letters and their variants will precede uppercase variants. Numeric values will precede all letter variants.

Before we move on to running queries against our views, let's walk through our earlier MapReduce example where we tried to count beer types by category. Start by clicking on the **Views** tab, where you'll now see you have the ability to add a view to your existing design document, as shown here:

Click on **Add View** in the line where the `dev_beers` design document is shown. Name this view `by_category`. Click on **Edit** next to the new view to return to the view editor page. Modify the map function so that it looks like this snippet:

```
function(doc, meta) {
  if (doc.type == "beer" &&doc.category) {
    emit(doc.category, 1);
  }
}
```

> This map function is the similar to the function we wrote earlier in this chapter, but it now includes a safety check so that beers without a category are not indexed. Without the null check, the index would contain numerous documents that do not have a category. Checking for a property's existence is a common practice when creating views.

Once you've modified the view code, click on **Save**. Then click on **Show Results**. The grid should look similar to that of our `by_name` index, but with the addition of `1` to the value for each indexed document, as shown next:

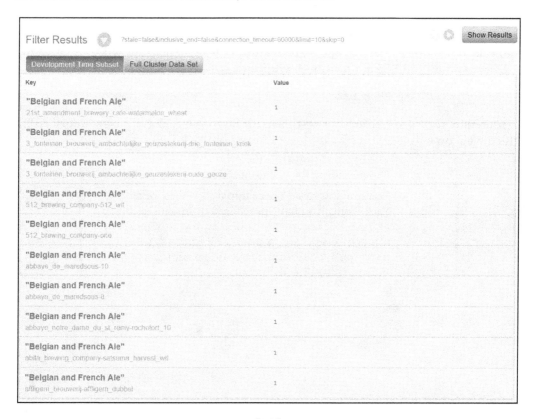

Take note of the fact that at this point, each category appears in our results, once for each beer with which it's associated. To find the count of beers grouped by category, we'll need to add a reduce function to our view. For this example, simply use the built-in _count function in the reduce editor. After you've made that change, click on **Save** and then on **Show Results**. You can see the following result:

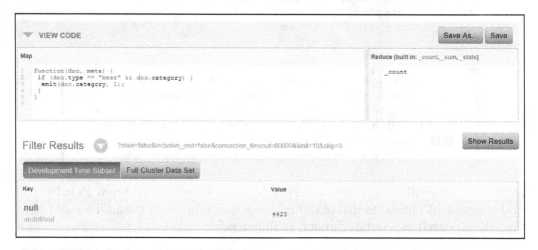

The results you see might not be what you expected. We've said all along that our goal was to provide a count of beers grouped by category. Instead, what we're seeing is the equivalent of a SQL COUNT query without a GROUP BY clause:

```
SELECT COUNT(*) FROM Beers
```

To understand how we group our results, we'll have to explore the view query API, which we'll do in the next section.

Downloading the example code

You can download the example code files for all Packt books you have purchased from your account at http://www.packtpub.com. If you purchased this book elsewhere, you can visit http://www.packtpub.com/support and register to have the files e-mailed directly to you.

Querying views

An important distinction to make at this point is that views are not queries, but means of querying for documents. You'll run queries against the view index in order to find the original documents. It is a common misconception that the views you write are actual queries.

Couchbase views have an API that supports a variety of search options, from an exact key search to a key range search. Continuing to use the Couchbase Console, we'll explore the various parameters we are able to use as we query our views. Begin by clicking on the down arrow next to the **Filter Results** text above the results panel.

Filtering views

Grouping

To continue with the reduce example, check the box next to **group** and click on **Close**. Click on **Show Results** again, and you'll now see that the results are grouped by the name of the category, as shown here:

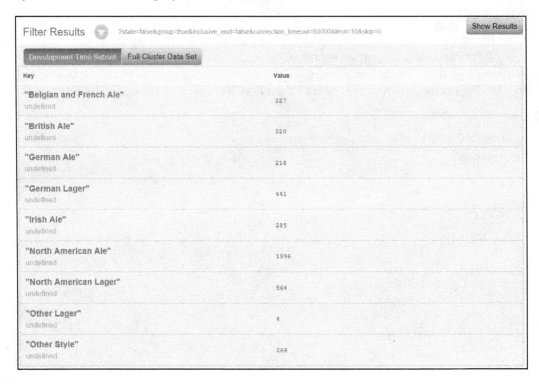

There's an additional parameter called **group_level** under the **group** option. This parameter takes an integer argument and is meant to be used with composite (array) keys. Our map function produces only a single-value key, so we'll avoid exploring this option until *Chapter 4, Advanced Views*.

Key queries

To continue our examination of the different view query options, let's return to our by_name view. Scroll up to the top of the page and select this view from the drop-down list. You can see this in the following screenshot:

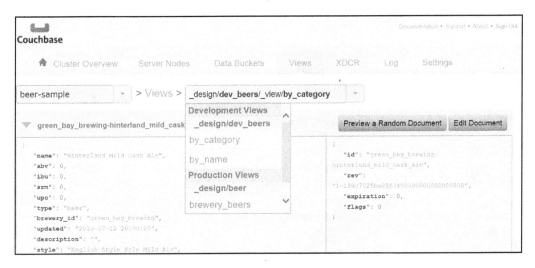

Once the page has refreshed with the by_name view, return to the **Filter Results** section and expand the dialog. For our first query, we'll search for beer types with names starting with the letters *B* and *C*. To do so, enter `"B"` in the **startkey** field and `"D"` in the **endkey** field. Note that the quotes around your start and end keys must be included.

Close the dialog and click on **Show Results** again. You'll see that the first beer types shown have names starting with the letter *B*. You can click all over the list to see the results that were returned as part of our view query.

 Note that if you page through the list, you might not find a beer starting with *C*. The reason is that the results view panel limits your results to only 100 records.

Range queries such as these are useful when we don't know exactly what we're looking for. However, we'll often want to search for a document by an exact match on an indexed property. To achieve this result, simply supply a string value to the **key** parameter, such as `"Three Philosophers"` or `"(512) ALT"`. Similarly, if you want to search on multiple keys in one query, you can supply an array to the **keys** parameter, such as `["Three Philosophers", "(512) ALT"]`.

Eventual consistency

We'll explore the parameters that we saw in the previous section, along with other parameters, in more detail in the next chapter. One last parameter we'll examine now is the `stale` option. You've already learned that views are incrementally updated, which means your query might be against a stale view. In other words, if a document was modified, the current state of the index might not have considered that change yet.

This delay between the time a document is modified and the time it is indexed is known as **eventual consistency**. In other words, the right or current value for a document will eventually be made consistent in the view index. In many cases this might be acceptable, but for others it's not. Fortunately, with Couchbase you can tune your consistency requirements for views.

By default, querying a view will trigger an update to the index after the results of the query are returned. This is done by the `update_after` argument, which may be supplied to the `stale` parameter. If you need a fully consistent answer, then set the `stale` value to `false`. If stale data is permissible, set the `stale` value to `ok`. This last option will not force an update of the view index.

> Prior to Couchbase Server 3.0, a document had to be made to persist in the disk before it could be considered for an index. This meant that true consistency between in-memory documents and view indexes required a combination of key/value operation with a `stale` value of `false`. Couchbase Server 3.0 introduces new stream-based views. Built on the new **Data Change Protocol** (**DCP**), streamed views may be made consistent by setting `stale` to `false`. This setting considers in-memory changes.

Couchbase SDKs and views

For another perspective on your view, click on the link right above the grid of results. This link will lead to a JSON view of our index:

```
{
    "total_rows": 5891,
    "rows": [
        {
            "id": "sullivan_s_black_forest_brew_haus_grill",
            "key": ".38 Special Bitter",
            "value": null
        },
        {
```

```
        "id": "512_brewing_company-512_alt",
        "key": "(512) ALT",
        "value": null
    },
    {

        "id": "512_brewing_company-512_bruin",
        "key": "(512) Bruin",
        "value": null

    }
  ]
}
```

The client libraries will use this JSON when querying a view. This view also introduces an important element of the Couchbase Server view API—the fact that it's HTTP-based. Unlike the key/value API, which is a binary protocol, views are queried over a RESTful API, with parameter values supplied as query string arguments. Being able to see the JSON that your client library sees is useful not only for debugging but also for understanding how you'll work with views through your SDK.

Unlike documents, which reside in memory (when available), view indexes are stored in the disk. Therefore, it's more expensive to query a view than to retrieve a document by its key. As such, it is best practice to think of an index as a means to retrieve the document's key. Once the key is found, you'll then use the key/value API to retrieve the original document.

 It is a common mistake to output the original document as a part of the map function by supplying doc as the value argument to emit (). Doing so means storing a copy of your document with the index, which will not be kept in sync with the doc argument in the memory.

As you can see in the previous JSON, each record in the index provides your SDK with three values. The first parameter, "id", is the key for a document to use with the key/value API. The second parameter, "key", is the key that was indexed. Your queries are made against this key. The third parameter, "value", is the value you output, typically to be used with reduce.

To see how you can use an SDK to query a view, consider the following C# snippet:

```
var query = bucket.CreateQuery("dev_beers", "by_name");
var result = bucket.Query<dynamic>(query);
foreach (var item in result.Rows)
{
  Console.WriteLine(item.Key);
}
```

In this example, the client SDK will query the view (without arguments) and get back an enumerable `View` object. As the view is iterated over, the `GetItem()` method uses the index row's `id` property to query for the original document via the key/value API. The Java SDK has a similar approach:

```
View view = client.getView("beer", "brewery_beers");
Query query = new Query();
query.setKeys("[\"Three Philosophers\",\"(512) ALT\"]");
ViewResponse response = client.query(view, query);
for (ViewRow row : response) {
System.out.println(row.getDocument());
}
```

Each SDK adheres to roughly the same pattern. First, you get access to a view object of some type and set any parameters you need to set. Then you iterate over the results, getting the original document by the ID value found in the index.

For better performance, you should consider using the multi-get operations. To do so, you should first aggregate the set of `id` values into some enumerable structure, and then pass that set of IDs to the multi-get operation of the SDK. The following C# snippet demonstrates how to create a list of IDs from the view results and then supply those IDs to a multi-get operation:

```
var query = bucket.CreateQuery("dev_beers", "by_name");
var result = bucket.Query<dynamic>(query);
var ids = result.Rows.Select(r =>r.Id).ToList();
var beers = bucket.Get<dynamic>(ids);
```

Summary

We covered a lot of ground in this chapter. In the beginning, you saw Couchbase only as a key/value store. Since then, you learned that Couchbase is a very capable document store as well, treating JSON documents as first-class citizens.

You learned the purpose of secondary indexes in a key/value store. We dug deep into MapReduce, both in terms of its history in functional languages and as a tool for NoSQL and big data systems.

As far as Couchbase MapReduce is concerned, we only scratched the surface. While you learned how to develop, test, and query views, the queries covered so far were simple. Couchbase view queries are capable of a lot more, which you will see as we move forward.

In the next chapter, we'll cover MapReduce in detail. We will have to start exploring more complex views, with a special focus on queries you're probably used to in SQL. From complex keys to simulating joins, you'll soon see that Couchbase views can be used for a lot more than simple queries.

4
Advanced Views

In the previous chapter, we explored the basics of the view API in Couchbase Server. Having spent a fair bit of time discussing MapReduce, we're now ready to move on to more advanced views. In this chapter, we'll dig deep into most of the common application queries you'll likely need to build an application with Couchbase.

Querying by type

One of the most basic tasks when building applications is to find all records of a particular type. In the relational world, this effort is analogous to SELECT * FROM TableName. For example, you might need to display a list of all users in your system. For this query, we aren't concerned with any particular attribute of a document other than that it is a user document:

```
function (doc, meta) {
  if (doc.type == "user") {
    emit(null, null);
  }
}
```

In this example, we'll simply check for the "user" type, and then emit a null key for each user document that is found. Since we didn't check for any property values other than the type, the index will contain all user documents. Again, the previous map function is similar to a SELECT * SQL query without a WHERE clause:

```
var view = client.GetView("users", "all_users");
foreach(var row in view)
{
  var user = row.GetItem() as User;
//do something with the user
}
```

In the preceding C# snippet, the `all_users` view from the `users` design document is queried with no arguments. As the view object is enumerated, each document is retrieved by its key or value (performed by the `GetItem()` method).

You're likely wondering why we emitted a null value for the key in our map function. Recall that every row in a Couchbase view contains the ID or key from the key/value API as a part of its data structure. Therefore, it would be redundant to include a value for the key. The `id` property is exposed to the SDKs when they query the view over the RESTful view API:

```
{"id":"user_12345","key":null,"value":null}
```

Another point to remember is that Couchbase documents are not namespaced beyond the bucket level. There is no table analogy. As such, for a "find all" query such as the one we saw before (to find all users), some sort of convention is required to identify the type of the document. In this case, we're using the convention of having a type property with each document, as we saw in *Chapter 3, Creating Secondary Indexes with Views*.

Finally, it's worth mentioning again that the purpose of a view is to provide a way of accessing the original document over the key/value API. If you know a document's key from its key/value API, you wouldn't use a view to find it. You'll use views to find keys for documents when those keys are not immediately or easily known.

Nested collections

So far, we've focused on pretty simple documents. In practice, however, you're more likely to work with complex JSON structures that mirror your application's object graph. For example, consider the common `Customer` class. In this case, you have a `Customer` object, which has a collection of `Address` objects, as demonstrated in the following C# snippet:

```csharp
public class Customer
{
    public string FirstName { get; set; }
    public string LastName { get; set; }
    public IEnumerable<Address> Addresses { get; set; }
}

public class Address
{
    public string Street { get; set; }
    public string City { get; set; }
    public string Province { get; set; }
```

```
    public string State { get; set; }
    public string Country { get; set; }
    public string PostalCode { get; set; }
}
```

In a relational model, this object structure would translate into a one-to-many relationship between a `Customers` table and an `Addresses` table. By contrast, with document databases, you tend to store related object graphs in the same document. As such, your JSON structure would look something like this sample:

```
{
    firstName = "Paulie",
    lastName = "Walnuts",
    type = "customer"
    addresses = [
        {
            street: "20 Mulberry Street",
            city: "Newark",
            state: "NJ",
            postalCode: "07102",
            country: "US"
        },
        {
            street: "10 Ridge Street",
            city: "Orange",
            state: "NJ",
            postalCode: "07050",
            country: "US"
        }
    ]
}
```

Our JSON resembles our in-memory object graph much more closely than it does the relational equivalent. However, in the relational world, finding all customers who live in a given state or have a given postal code is possible with a straightforward query:

```
SELECT *
FROM Addresses a
INNER JOIN Customers c ON c.Id = a.CustomerId
WHERE State = 'NJ'
```

Fortunately, the map function that allows a similar query to be run is not as complex as those we've seen already. The only real difference is that we'll loop over the nested collection and emit the index values from within that loop, as follows:

```
function(doc, meta) {
    if (doc.type == "customer" && doc.addresses) {
      for(vari = 0; i<doc.addresses.length; i++) {
        if (doc.addresses[i].state) {
          emit(doc.addresses[i].state, null);
        }
      }
    }
}
```

This map function also demonstrates that within a map multiple properties or objects from the same document may be indexed. For each address in a `customer` document, there will be a corresponding record in the index.

Now we can see that, since our map function is simply a JavaScript function, we can do in our map function virtually anything that we can do in JavaScript. You are able to create quite complex map functions, including having the ability to create anonymous functions.

 It is a common question as to whether you're able to include JavaScript libraries to be used in your map and reduce functions. Practically speaking, you aren't. You could probably manage to wedge jQuery into a map function, but that would be quite impractical.

It's not always right to nest related entities as we just did with customer addresses. There are times when it will make more sense to store a related record in its own document. For example, you probably wouldn't want to nest products purchased by a customer within the customer record. Instead, you would likely store a reference to a product document's key. In *Chapter 6, Designing a Schema-less Data Mode*, we'll explore these patterns in more detail.

Range queries

We've seen the basics of key range queries but haven't fully explored how they work. Understanding range queries is critical in order to understand how to perform a number of common query tasks. We'll start by revisiting a basic range query. We'll use a simple document structure, as shown here:

```
{
  "firstName": "Hank",
  "lastName": "Moody",
  "type": "user"
},
{
  "firstName": "Karen",
  "lastName": "Van Der Beek",
  "type": "user"
},
{
  "firstName": "Becca",
  "lastName": "Moody-Smith",
  "type": "user"
}
```

In this example, we have three documents. We'll start by writing the map function, which will allow us to perform queries by last name. This is our standard view definition with a check on type and for the existence of a lastName property:

```
function (doc, meta) {
  if (doc.type == "user" && doc.lastName) {
    emit(doc.lastName, null);
  }
}
```

As a refresher, to find a user by the last name, we'll simply provide the value "Moody" as a view parameter (including the quotes). That is a basic key search. But what if we wanted to find all Moody records, even those with a hyphenated last name? In this case, we can use a range query.

To query a view by a range, there are two parameters to be set, startkey and endkey. Even with that knowledge in mind, it might still not be obvious what values to provide for these parameters. The startkey parameter represents the lower bounds of the range, and the endkey parameter represents the upper bounds. It might be obvious how you'd perform a range query on integers, but how do you perform a range query on words?

Deliberately taking a naïve approach, we'll start by using `"M"` and `"N"` as our arguments for `startkey` and `endkey`, respectively. While with our limited dataset we'd certainly get both the Moody records, we'd also get any document with a last name starting with the letter M.

As a second step, we could change `startkey` to `"Moody"`. While this would eliminate documents such as one with a last name of Matthews, it would leave records such as Morissette. The question then becomes, what are the values greater than Moody? More specifically, we want to find values greater than Moody followed by a hyphen, and any other name. Before we look at the answer, let's first revisit the notion of Unicode collation.

When we compare strings in most programming languages, we tend to rely on ASCII or byte order. In byte order, A is less than (or ordered before) a, but greater than B. By contrast, with Unicode Collation, a is less than A and less than B, which is greater than b. Additionally, accented variants are also grouped together with letters. For example, a is less than à, and A is less than Ã. The following example illustrates the basics of Unicode sorting:

```
1 < 5 < a < à < A < Ã < c < ç < C
```

Now that we have understood how view results are sorted, we can solve the problem of ending our range query. What we want is a value that will always be higher than any last name starting with Moody followed by a hyphen. This value should also be less than any value that could be greater than Moody followed by a hyphen.

With Couchbase server, the practice is to create an upper bound that starts with the values you hope to match, but suffixes that value with some high-order value. For example, one approach would be to set `startkey` to `"Moody"` and `endkey` to `"Moody-ZZZZ"`. While this approach is likely to catch most documents, what about last names starting with Z, or any other accented Z character?

A better approach is to select a boundary outside the likely realm of possible values for a name. Usually, this approach involves using the value at the end of the Unicode Collation table, which is `\u02ad`. Therefore, if we want to capture all "Moody-?" names, we'd use an `endkey` parameter of `"Moody-\u02ad"`.

> Note that in this example, the last name moody would not be part of the query results because m is less than M. To address this issue, we can either change the query to have a start range of moody or modify the map function to emit all lowercase keys.

It's also worth mentioning that this type of query is effectively a "starts with" or LIKE "A%" query. In other words, it provides a means of searching for all documents that start with a particular string. There is no comparable "ends with" query.

Multiple keys per document

The preceding map function we just wrote has a limitation—it will identify only those last names where the desired name appears before the hyphen. Therefore, the last name Van Der Beek-Moody would not be found. To address this issue, we could query a second time, with the startkey and endkey parameters reversed from our previous query. However, there is a better way.

There is no rule that a document must have only one key per row in an index. Therefore, we can rewrite our index to emit an index row for every possible last name. In this example, a possible last name is anything appearing before or after a hyphen:

```
function(doc, meta) {
  if (doc.type == "user" && doc.lastName) {
    var parts = doc.lastName.split("-");
    for(vari = 0; i<parts.length; i++) {
      emit(parts[i], null);
    }
  }
}
```

In this new map function, we use JavaScript's string split() function to return each of the names contained in a last name. For each match name we find, we send it to the index. Now the document with a last name of Moody-Smith will have two rows in the index, one for Moody and one for Smith. The Van Der Beek-Moody document will also have two rows.

This approach is far more powerful because it allows us to perform a key query rather than a key range query. To find all Moody documents, we simply set the key parameter's value to "Moody" (with the quotes). Regardless of where Moody appears in the last name, it will be found by our query.

As another example, consider a blog post document where the post includes a set of tags. You want to be able to locate all the posts with the same tag:

```
{
  "title" : "About  Couchbase Views",
  "body" : "Views are secondary indexes...",
  "type" : "post",
  "tags" : ["couchbase", "nosql", "views"]
}
```

In this example, the `tags` property is an array of strings. The map function used to index these tags will be similar to the function we just wrote to index last names in our user documents:

```
function(doc, meta) {
  if (doc.type == "post" && doc.tags && doc.tags,length) {
    for(vari = 0; i<doc.tags.length; i++) {
      emit(doc.tags[i], null);
    }
  }
}
```

Since our tags were already stored in an array, all we need to do is iterate over those values and emit them to the index. Note that we'll also verify that our document has a `tags` property and that the `tags` property has a `length` property. This test will ensure that even if the document has a `tags` property, it is also an enumerable property, such as an array.

As another example of this approach to indexing documents, consider the goal of indexing the words in a document's `title` property. Our goal is to create a simple text index:

```
function(doc, meta) {
  if (doc.type == "post" && doc.title) {
    var words = doc.title.split(" ");
    for(vari = 0; i<words.length; i++) {
      emit(doc.words[i], null);
    }
  }
}
```

Simply splitting the words in the title and emitting them to an index allows us to query for documents by words in the post's `title`. Of course, if a true full-text index is what you need, you'd likely want to use a full-text search tool such as **Elasticsearch**. Fortunately, the Couchbase team supplies an Elasticsearch plugin. It can be used to push data from a Couchbase cluster to an Elasticsearch cluster. The plugin is available for download at `http://www.couchbase.com/nosql-databases/downloads`.

The final example of emitting multiple keys per document demonstrates how to emulate an OR query. Using our user documents, we'll emit an index that includes both first and last names. In SQL, this query would be similar to the following:

```
SELECT *
FROM Users
WHERE LastName = 'Moody' OR FirstName = 'Hank'
```

For the map function, we'll simply add an extra call to emit so that both first and last names are sent:

```
function(doc, meta) {
  if (doc.type == "user" && doc.firstName && doc.lastName) {
    emit(doc.firstName, null);
    emit(doc.lastName, null);
  }
}
```

The index will consist of two rows for each user document, one for the first name and one for the last name. To run an OR query, you would use the keys parameter, supplying an array of the values that you want to search, for example ["Hank", "Moody"].

Querying a view by keys yields all the documents that match the supplied keys. Keys that don't match are ignored (much like OR). One thing to keep in mind is that in this approach, you aren't specifying whether a key is a first name or last name, as would be the case with SQL. We'll learn how to enhance this view in the next section.

It's good practice to check for null any and all properties being emitted to an index. Such checks make it safer to perform actions on your emitted properties, or to have reduce functions that won't encounter unexpected null values. The following snippet could break your indexing if lastName were null:

```
emit(doc.lastName.toLowerCase(),null);
```

Compound indexes

Writing an AND query requires a different approach than what we used for our OR query. If you wanted to perform the analogue of a SQL query with multiple values in a WHERE clause, you'd need to structure your view keys in such a way as to allow your application to supply multiple values as one key parameter value:

```
SELECT *
FROM Users
WHERE LastName = 'Soprano' AND FirstName = 'Tony'
```

In the preceding SQL statement, we are able to have values for both LastName and FirstName. One approach would be to create a delimited key in our index like this:

```
function(doc, meta) {
  if (doc.type == "user" && doc.firstName && doc.lastName) {
    emit(doc.lastName + "," + doc.firstName, null);
  }
}
```

This map function emits a key in the form of "Soprano, Tony" to the index. When querying the index, the client application would concatenate the last name, a comma, and the first name. The resulting string would be provided as the argument for the key parameter.

Obviously, it's not optimal to concatenate a set of values in order to run a query. Fortunately, as we saw briefly in *Chapter 3, Creating Secondary Indexes with Views*, Couchbase views support compound indexes. Recall that compound indexes are simply array keys. With this change in mind, we could rewrite the last name and first name indexes in this way:

```
function(doc, meta) {
  if (doc.type == "user" && doc.firstName && doc.lastName) {
    emit([doc.lastName, doc.firstName], null);
  }
}
```

In this version of the map function, we have an array key where the last name is the first element and the first name is the second element. With this change, when a client queries for a combination of first and last names, the key parameter is used. The key to search on will be a valid JSON array, for example, ["Moody", "Hank"]. On the client side, no concatenation is required.

Grouping keys

The real power of composite keys isn't the ability to search in multiple fields, but the ability to perform grouping with aggregation. To illustrate this point, we'll revisit the blog post document with a new property for published date:

```
{
    "title": "Composite Keys with Couchbase Views ",
    "body": "Composite keys are arrays...",
    "publishedDate": "2014-09-17",
    "type": "post"
}
```

Let's imagine that we want to display both a list of posts by year and month and the count of posts by year and month. By writing a view that uses compound keys and grouping methods, we are able to achieve both. Starting with the map function, we'll emit the year and month as values in our composite (array) key:

```
function(doc, meta) {
    if (doc.type == "post" &&doc.publishedDate) {
        emit(dateToArray(doc.publishedDate), null);
    }
}
```

As always, we first check the type of the document and verify that it contains a `publishedDate` property. We then use the built-in `dateToArray` function provided by Couchbase. This is quite useful because JSON doesn't define a date type.

This function will take a document date string and provide the constituent pieces as items in an array, for example `2014-09-17` becomes `[2014, 9, 17, 0, 0, 0]`. Then we can see that each of our keys will be an array of integers, starting with the year, followed by the month, then the day, and then the time components.

We'll start by getting a count of posts by year. To do so, we'll need to add a reduce function to our view. We'll simply use the built-in `_count` function. Additionally, we'll need to make use of the `group_level` parameter. If we provide `1` as an argument to `group_level`, the view results will be grouped by the first item of the array index. In SQL, you could think of this behavior as a `SELECT COUNT(*)` statement:

```
SELECT Year, Count(*)
FROM posts
GROUP BY Year
```

As you can probably guess, to get a count of posts by month, we'd simply change the `group_level` to 2. It's important to understand that group levels are always inclusive of the elements in earlier positions in the array. In other words, when you group results at level 2 (that is, month), level 1 (year) is always considered. In SQL, grouping at level 2 would be analogous to the following statement:

```
SELECT Year, Month, Count(*)
FROM posts
GROUP BY Year, Month
```

If you wanted to group results by months across all years, you will need to write a separate view that emits the month as the first element in the array. In this case, you will not be able to use the built-in `dateToArray` helper function directly in the emit call. You can use the result of the `dateToArray` function, but you should omit the year when emitting the key.

When you supply a group level, the keys against which you would perform range queries are no longer the fully emitted arrays, but rather the arrays at the specified level, for example at level 2, `[2014,3,23,0,0,0]` becomes `[2014,3]`. At group level 1, the index includes only the year.

You query compound keys with range arguments. You provide `startkey` and `endkey`, as we saw earlier in this chapter. However, with compound keys, you will provide arrays as the values passed to these parameters. If you wanted to find the count of posts by month for the first half of a year, you could provide a `startkey` value of `[2014]` and an `endkey` value of `[2014,6,99]`.

Assuming you're familiar with the Gregorian calendar, you probably noticed that the upper bound of date was not valid — June has only 30 days. This value illustrates an important aspect of how composite keys are treated when queried. Specifically, queries are not performed against arrays but rather concatenated strings (from the array values) are used.

Recall the discussion earlier in this chapter about Unicode collation. Compound key queries are compared in the same way. While it seems that we've created a set of keys as integer arrays, Couchbase actually maintains those keys as strings. More specifically, Couchbase Server will treat all the array characters as elements in the strings, including brackets and commas. Additionally, single digits will be padded with a leading zero.

Therefore, when you set the `startkey` and `endkey` parameters to `[2014]` and `[2014,6,99]` respectively, the actual comparison is made by comparing the strings passed to these parameters to the `["2014"]` and `["2014","06","31"]` key parameter strings. In this case, `[2014]` will always be less than any date with a month, including January 1, and also 99 will always be greater than any possible day of June (`"06"`) will always be less than July (`"07"`).

If we omit the `group_level` parameter entirely but leave the key ranges in place, we'll be provided with an ungrouped list of all posts over that time period. Instead, if we want to get a list of posts for a given month, we should again leave the `group_level` parameter, but supply a shorter range for our `startkey` and `endkey` parameters. In both of our ungrouped cases, it is also necessary to add set the `reduce` parameter to `false`.

Emitting values

Up until this point, we've written most of our map functions to emit null for the value side of our key/value views. We've also learnt that it's best to use views as a means to retrieve a document via the key/value API. However, there are exceptions to this rule.

Imagine that we've augmented our user documents to include an e-mail address, like this:

```
{
    "firstName": "Sam",
    "lastName": "Malone",
    "email": "sam@example.com",
    "type": "user"
}
```

Now consider the task of creating some sort of scheduled job that needs to send a weekly e-mail to all users. We've already seen how to write the "select all users" query. Therefore, we know how to iterate over the set of users and retrieve the original user document to get this new e-mail property. However, this isn't necessarily the most efficient way to do so.

If we have millions of user documents, we'd be querying both the view and key/value API millions of times. By emitting the e-mail address as the value in our index, we can turn our index into what is called a **Covering Index** in the SQL world. Such an index is able to answer a query with the index data alone:

```
//the map function for a view named by_lastname
function(doc, meta) {
```

```
        if (doc.type == "user" && doc.email&&doc.lastName) {
            emit(doc.lastName, doc.email);
        }
    }
```

In this code snippet, our `by_lastname` view has been re-purposed to include e-mail as a value. In doing so, some space on disk is saved by not having an entirely separate index for e-mail. Also, some resources are saved by not having an extra indexing job on the server.

In deciding whether to include a value with your view, space and data freshness will be the important factors. If you are including large chunks of your document in your index, you'd instead want to use the key/value lookup pattern. Similarly, if the data you are emitting to your view needs to be fully up to date, you should again use the key/value lookup, even if the data stored is small.

It's also worth noting that values (as well as keys) do not need to be primitive types or strings. It is possible (and sometimes desirable) to emit a JSON structure. For example, imagine our user document is much larger than the small snippet we've seen. We're frequently going to query user documents through views, but we'll need to access the full document less frequently:

```
function(doc, meta) {
    if (doc.type == "user"&&doc.email&&doc.firstName&&doc.lastName)
    {
        emit(doc.email, { "firstName": doc.firstName,
"lastName": doc.lastName });
    }
}
```

In the preceding map function, we assume a use case where we'll frequently look up a user by e-mail and then retrieve their first and last names. Again, storing values with your index when you're not reducing the amount of data retrieved generally comes at a cost. It's far more common to emit a value with a reduce function.

Imagine we have a set of order documents where each order includes a price:

```
{
    "customerId" : "123456",
    "products": [
        {
            "product": "fender_telecaster",
            "price": 1249.99
        },
        {
            "product": "line6_spider",
```

```
        "price": 299.99
      }
    ],
    "type": "order"
  }
```

If we wanted to calculate a total of all purchases by a customer, we would emit the price as a value and use the built-in _sum function as our reduce function:

```
function(doc, meta) {
  if (doc.type == "order" && doc.products&&doc.products.length) {
    for(vari = 0; i<doc.products.length; i++) {
      emit(doc.customerId, doc.products[i].price);
    }
  }
}
```

This map function emits a separate index row for each product purchased in a specific order. Alternatively, we could have computed the order total in our loop and emitted a single row with just that order's total.

When we query this view, we need to include the group parameter as well as the reduce parameter (both true). The result will be similar to the following SQL statement. In the relational world, we'd have a separate table for line items unlike our document, which nests each ordered product within the order document:

```
SELECT CustomerId, SUM(Price)
FROM OrderItems
GROUP BY CustomerId
```

Querying with beer-sample

So far, we've explored a wide variety of view queries. For some more concrete examples, we'll turn now to the **beer-sample** bucket. If you followed along in *Chapter 3, Creating Secondary Indexes with Views*, you should already have a design document created in this bucket. If so, then feel free to reuse that document. If not, then you'll need to create a new document.

Start by returning to the **Views** tab on the Couchbase Web Console. Select the **beer-sample** bucket to retrieve the current set (if any) of views within the dev_beers design document. If you did not follow along in the previous chapter, refer to the *Creating a view* section in *Chapter 3, Creating Secondary Indexes with Views* to get started. The following screenshot shows the Couchbase Console's **Views** tab:

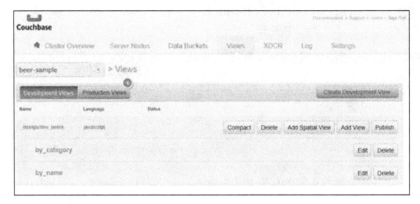

The Couchbase Console Views tab

Querying all documents by type

We'll start by revisiting the first view we looked at in this chapter — querying for all documents of a given type. Our first approach was to create an index with null keys and values for all user documents. This approach works well for organizing your design documents in a manner similar to your application's business objects.

Another option would be to create a single view which will allow you to search for all documents of any type. To achieve this goal, we'll simply emit each document's type property to the keys of the index:

```
function (doc, meta) {
  if (doc.type) {
    emit(doc.type, null);
  }
}
```

With this version of our SELECT * view, every document with a type property will have a corresponding row in the index. When we want to query for all beers, we simply provide the key property as "beer", or the "brewery" parameter for breweries. This is shown in the following screenshot:

Finding all brewery documents

Counting breweries by location

Brewery documents in the **beer-sample** bucket contain address information. With these properties, we're able to write a view to count the number of breweries in a country, state, or province, down to the postal code level. Because the sample data often lack postal codes, we'll stop at the city level.

Our map function will be fairly straightforward. We'll emit an array as the key where the values of the array are the document's country, city, state, and code properties. The following map function produces keys such as ["Belgium","Hainaut","Binche"] and ["Canada","Quebec","Chambly"]:

```
function(dsoc, meta) {
  if (doc.type == "brewery" &&doc.country&&doc.state&&doc.city)
{
  emit([doc.country, doc.state, doc.city], null);
  }
}
```

To get a count of breweries by country, we first need to add a reduce function. Just as we have done before, we'll use the built-in _count function. After saving the view with the reduce function in place, we'll need to set the group_level parameter to 1, as shown here:

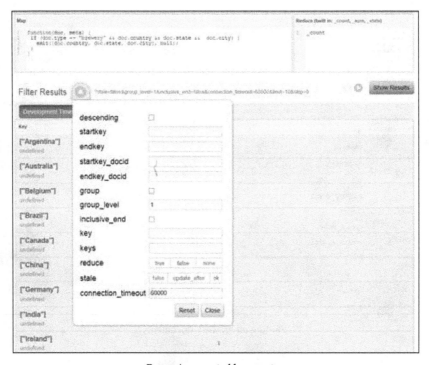

Breweries counted by country

Similarly, we could set the group_level parameter to 2 or 3 to get a count of breweries by province or city, respectively, as shown in the following screenshot. Recall that group_level is always inclusive of the previous levels. We can't count breweries in Connecticut without including the United States. Similarly, we can't count breweries in Hartford without including both Connecticut and the United States.

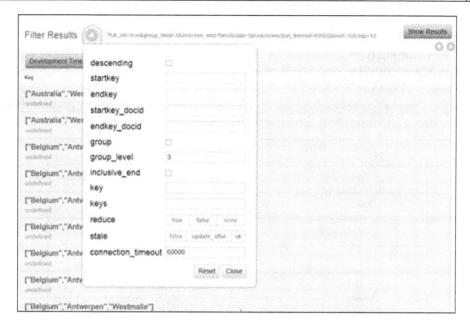

If you're a beer aficionado, you might find the sample data to be lacking in some of your favorite brews. This is because the source of the brewery data was the **Open Beer Database**, which is no longer maintained. Moreover, many of the documents have incomplete address components. Keep these limitations in mind as you pull back results that suggest Ireland has only one brewery.

If we want to find out how many breweries exist for a specific city, we will need to provide `startkey` and `endkey`. The approach we'll take will be the same as the approach we used to find blog posts by a specific month. For the `startkey` parameter, we'll provide an exact country and state, for example, `["United States", "Massachusetts"]`.

For an `endkey` value, we'll need to supply a value that is greater than all possible city values in Massachusetts. In this case, it would probably be safe to use a `startkey` value such as `["United States", "Massachusetts", "ZZZZ"]` since no city in Massachusetts (or anywhere else) is ever likely to be given a value greater than `"ZZZZ"`. However, it's safer to use an `endkey` value in the form of `["United States", "Massachusetts", "\u02ad"]`, as `\u02ad` will always be greater than any city name. The following screenshot demonstrates this example:

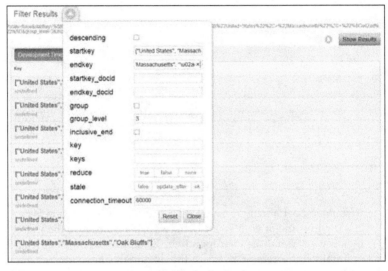

Counting breweries by state

While we are unable to reuse this view to query for breweries by country or state, it may be used to find breweries in a particular city. To accomplish this task, simply remove the `reduce` parameter (or set it to `false`) and perform a `key` query, such as `["United States", "Massachusetts", "Cambridge"]`, as shown here:

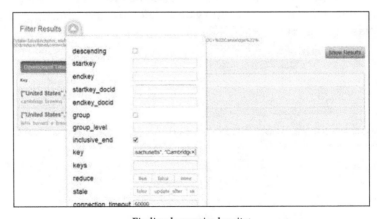

Finding breweries by city

This type of view is useful to work with any set of hierarchical properties. With this example, we could have a page that shows a list of countries with brewery counts. Clicking on a country could then display a list of states, provinces and their brewery counts. Then, clicking on a state would show a list of cities and brewery counts. Finally, clicking on a city would show all the breweries in that city.

Finding beer documents by brewery

To understand how to look up a beer name by its brewery, we first need to examine the relationship between the two types of documents. Recall that Couchbase Server does not support foreign keys and there is no referential integrity between documents. However, it is common to create a relationship by adding a property to a foreign document.

Each beer document contains a `brewery_id` property, and it is the `meta.id` property of a brewery document. Again, the `meta.id` value is the key from the key/value API. By including this property on beer documents, it's possible to write a simple map function to search for beer names by their brewery, as follows:

```
function(doc, meta) {
  if (doc.type == "beer" && doc.brewery_id) {
    emit(doc.brewery_id, null);
  }
}
```

Keep in mind that there are no joins in Couchbase Server. When you query this view with a `key` value such as `"pivzavod_baltika"`, you cannot get both the brewery and its beer document in a single lookup. Typically with Couchbase Server, you'll perform multiple `Get` operations to retrieve related documents.

Collated views

Though Couchbase Server does not support joins, there is a technique commonly used to find documents with a parent-child relationship. This technique is known as a **collated view** because it relies on Couchbase Server's Unicode collation. Before we dig into how we can build a collated view, it's useful to understand the goal.

We've already seen that Unicode collation guarantees that the index will be ordered by its key in a predictable and consumable way. In the previous section, we saw how to create an index of beer names where the key was the brewery's ID. That map function provides part of the solution—it orders all of a brewery's beer documents together.

The other part of the solution is to add the brewery document to the index alongside the beer documents. Specifically, we want a row with the brewery followed by each of its beer names. This technique is not obvious at first, so we'll take it piece by piece:

```
function(doc, meta) {
  if (doc.type == "brewery") {
    emit(meta.id);
  }
}
```

The preceding map function is fairly straightforward. We simply check for brewery documents and emit their `meta.id` value to the index. To add beer documents, we'll first modify the map function slightly, as follows:

```
function(doc, meta) {
  if (doc.type == "brewery") {
    emit(meta.id);
  } else if (doc.type == "beer" && doc.brewery_id) {
    emit(doc.brewery_id);
  }
}
```

We've added a second condition to our map function. Now if we encounter a beer document, we'll emit its `brewery_id` value as the key. At this point, we have an index entirely consisting of brewery IDs.

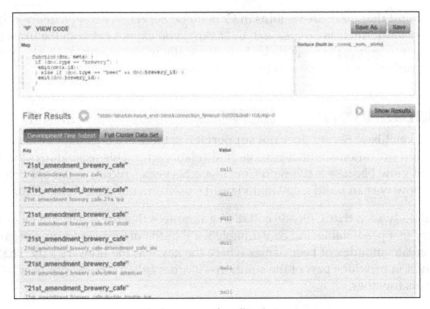

The beginning of a collated view

As we can see in the previous figure, our index consists of a brewery, followed by its beer names. In fact, all our beer names and breweries will appear in the index as brewery first and beer second. A client application can now query the view by brewery ID and build a set of parent-child objects.

Though it seems like we're done with our map function, we still have one final change to make. Even though our breweries correctly appear before the beer documents, it's only because of the way the beer keys were created in the **beer-sample** bucket.

Each beer's key (or `meta.id`) is prefixed with its brewery's key. Therefore, the brewery key will always be less than the beer key, for example the `"21st_amendment_brewery_cafe"` brewery key will always be less than its beer's keys (such as `" 21st_amendment_brewery_cafe-21a_ipa"`). Couchbase Server sorts results by the document's ID as a sort of tie-breaker for the same key in an index.

To fix our map function, we need to provide a means of forcing our parent rows to be emitted before any of its children rows, regardless of the `meta.id` value for its children. If we convert our keys to composite keys, we are easily able to enforce this ordering:

```
function(doc, meta) {
  if (doc.type == "brewery") {
    emit([meta.id, 0]);
  } else if (doc.type == "beer" && doc.brewery_id) {
    emit([doc.brewery_id, 1]);
  }
}
```

With this new map function in place, we emit 0 after the brewery's `meta.id` value, and 1 after the beer's `brewery_id` value. We've now guaranteed that all beer names will appear together immediately following their brewery. Moreover, the query to find a brewery with its beers simply requires `startkey` and `endkey` with the `brewery_id` value, followed by 0 and 1 respectively. The following screenshot demonstrates this example:

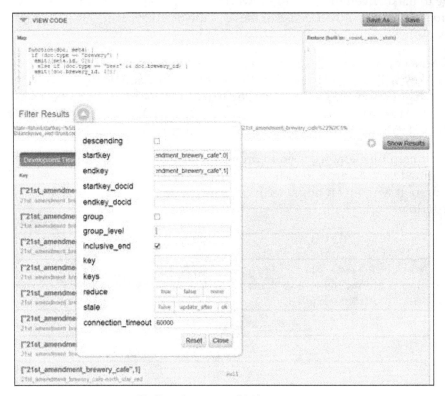

Finding a brewery and its beer names

Summary

Following the background information in *Chapter 3, Creating Secondary Indexes with Views*, you now saw a more complete picture of Couchbase views. You learned how a document can be indexed in virtually any way imaginable with JavaScript. Moreover, you now know that you can index a document in multiple ways within the same view.

Reviewing range queries led you to explore Unicode collation and some tricks to find your data. You also saw how you are able to parse collections within documents to create several indexed values from a single document field.

Then we explored compound indexes in some detail. You learned that these indexes provide so much more than grouping. We can use them to query multiple properties and to create an index that yields parent-child relationships.

Along the way, we alluded to some important topics. While discussing collated views, we touched on the importance of key (`meta.id`) selection for our documents. We also broached the subject of document relationships. These topics will resurface in more detail in *Chapter 6, Designing a Schema-less Data Model*, when we discuss schema design.

Before we move on to schema design, we're going to take a look at N1QL, an exciting new query language that is currently being developed by the Couchbase engineering team. Though it uses views behind the scenes, it offers a simpler approach to querying by providing a rich language to find data in a Couchbase bucket.

5
Introducing N1QL

After two chapters of exploring views and MapReduce, you might be wondering just how you would go about finding data in your bucket more easily. If you've worked with relational systems, you're likely used to being able to query your database ad hoc without having to create a stored procedure first. Having to write a view for one-off queries of your data probably seems less than optimal.

Fortunately, there is another option with Couchbase and it is known as **N1QL** (pronounced **nickel**). N1QL is a query language, reminiscent of SQL. Not only does it support ad hoc querying of your data, it also provides a means to perform joins and aggregation.

At the time of writing this book, N1QL is still in developer preview, though some Couchbase SDKs are starting to see support for it. We'll explore N1QL in some detail throughout this chapter, but keep in mind that with any prerelease product some changes are likely. However, the core concepts and interface are unlikely to see any drastic changes.

Installing N1QL

Couchbase Server does not ship with N1QL. It needs separate downloading and installation. As of **Developer Preview 3**, there are binaries for Windows, Red Hat Linux, and Mac OS X. You can find these packages at `http://www.couchbase.com/nosql-databases/downloads#PreRelease`. The package for your operating system will be in the form of a zipped archive.

It's important to remember that N1QL is still in developer preview and is not necessarily being kept in sync with all current Couchbase releases. While N1QL Developer Preview 3 does appear to work fine on Windows with Couchbase Server Community Edition 3.0.1, it will not work with Couchbase Server Enterprise Edition 3.0.2. If you are unable to complete the following tasks using the Enterprise Edition, you should try the Community Edition instead.

Once you've obtained the binaries for your system, you'll need to extract the contents. Expand (unzip) the archive to any location where you'll easily be able to get to via the command line. After extracting the files, navigate to that path and run the following command:

`./cbq-engine -couchbase http://localhost:8091`

This line attaches N1QL to your Couchbase Server instance. It will start a process that will listen on port 8093. After it starts, you should see output similar to this:

```
22:19:08.343741 Info line disabled false
22:19:08.348746 tuqtng started...
22:19:08.348746 version: v0.7.2
22:19:08.348746 site: http://localhost:8091
```

Once the cbq-engine is up and running, you're ready to start running N1QL queries against your buckets. The easiest way to do so is to run the command-line query interface, which can be found in the same directory as cbq-engine. You can run this tool using the following command:

`./cbq http://localhost:8093`

This command will open the cbq prompt where you are able to enter N1QL commands. In this chapter, we'll work with the **beer-sample** bucket. To prepare that bucket for queries, run this command from the cbq prompt:

`cbq> CREATE PRIMARY INDEX ON beer-sample`

With this step, you've actually created a view on the **beer-sample** bucket. If you open the Couchbase Console and navigate to the **Views** tab, you'll find a view named #primary contained within a ddl_#primary design document. Note that this design document will only appear under **Production Views**:

```
function (doc, meta) {
var stringToUtf8Bytes = function (str) {
var utf8 = unescape(encodeURIComponent(str));
var bytes = [];
```

```
    for (var i = 0; i<str.length; ++i) {
bytes.push(str.charCodeAt(i));
    }
    return bytes;
  };

  emit([160, stringToUtf8Bytes(meta.id)], null);
}
```

This relatively compact map function creates an index on document keys. You might be wondering why N1QL won't use a simpler map function, such as the following. After all, this map function also creates an index on document keys. The important distinction between N1QL queries and view queries is that view queries use the standard HTTP REST API and N1QL has its own query processor:

```
function (doc, meta) {
  emit(meta.id, null);
}
```

At this time, N1QL is simply taking advantage of the fact that indexes may be created using views. This coupling may very well change at some point. So, though the underlying facility to create indexes is the same between N1QL and MapReduce views, the actual querying is quite different and requires a different index key structure.

Having a primary index on a database simply means that primary keys have been indexed for use with N1QL. Just as in a relational database, if you were to query regularly by certain fields, it would be important to create indexes to avoid unnecessary scanning through documents.

For this chapter, we'll worry only about the primary index. If you want to experiment with creating other field indexes, the syntax is as follows. In this example, we create an index named by_abv on the abv field of documents in the **beer-sample** bucket:

```
CREATE INDEX by_abv ON beer-sample(abv)
```

With the primary index created, you're now ready to write your first N1QL query.

 If you're using Windows and its standard command line, you'll want to remove . / from the beginning of command-line examples. If you are using PowerShell on Windows or a Linux variant, you do not need to make any changes.

Simple queries

N1QL queries are likely to feel somewhat familiar to you as the language is very much like SQL and other such query languages. To illustrate just how similar N1QL and SQL are, consider the following query:

```
SELECT *
FROM beer-sample
```

This basic N1QL query looks and feels like the equivalent SQL query, and it does what you would expect it to do—it retrieves all documents from the **beer-sample** bucket. Recall that documents in a Couchbase bucket are not contained in a second-level namespace. As such, there is no equivalent of a SELECT * FROM Table statement.

Instead, if you want to find all brewery documents, you can write a N1QL query similar to the map function you would write in the case of a view. In both the cases, you have to check the convention-based type property to identify a document's taxonomy:

```
SELECT *
FROM beer-sample
WHERE type == "brewery"
```

Similarly, we can apply an additional WHERE clause to filter the results by another property before they are returned, as follows:

```
SELECT *
FROM beer-sample
WHERE type = "brewery"
AND country = "United States"
```

Again, there is virtually no difference between SQL and this N1QL query, save for the double quotes around strings. Even though you've seen only a couple of snippets of N1QL, it should be obvious that the Couchbase team designed N1QL to be immediately accessible to developers experienced with more traditional and relational systems.

As is the case with SQL, it's generally a good idea to project data from your queries rather than returning all properties in a document (or columns in the case of an RDBMS). Doing so with N1QL requires only that you specify the property names with your SELECT statement:

```
SELECT name
FROM beer-sample
WHERE type = "brewery"
AND country = "United States"
```

Ordering is also possible using familiar, SQL-like operations:

```
SELECT name
FROM beer-sample
WHERE type = "brewery"
ORDER BY name
```

Another common SQL task is limiting the number of results or skipping certain numbers of results before returning rows. Often, you'll do so to page results displayed on a client application. It is also possible to skip and limit with N1QL, as demonstrated in the following code. In this snippet, only 10 documents are returned, starting with the sixth. In other words, documents numbered six to 15 are returned:

```
SELECT *
FROM beer-sample
LIMIT 10 OFFSET 5
```

The default ordering of documents is based on the document's meta.id value. Recall that this is also the default ordering for a view where no explicit key is set (that is, emit(null, null);). To verify this ordering behavior, you can run the following query. This query uses the meta() function, which provides access to a document's metadata:

```
SELECT city, name, meta().id
FROM beer-sample
WHERE type = "brewery"
```

Should you wish to sort by a document's property, you may add the ORDER BY clause to your SELECT statement. Again, the syntax for this clause should be familiar to SQL developers, as shown in the following code. In this example, documents are sorted first in descending order by name, and then in ascending order by style:

```
SELECT *
FROM beer-sample
WHERE type = "beer"
ORDER BY name DESC, style
```

N1QL also provides a means to search for documents by document keys. This search is performed by adding a KEY (KEYS for multiple keys) clause to a SELECT statement. To search for a single item by key, you provide a single key:

```
SELECT *
FROM beer-sample
KEY "thomas_hooker_brewing"
```

Alternatively, you can search for multiple documents with multiple keys:

```
SELECT *
FROM beer-sample
KEYS [
"thomas_hooker_brewing-hooker_oktoberfest",
"thomas_hooker_brewing-thomas-hooker_irish_red_ale",
"thomas_hooker_brewing"
]
```

To remove duplicate results from a query result set, simply apply the DISTINCT keyword to the projected properties. For example, to retrieve the distinct set of countries with breweries, you can execute this query:

```
SELECT DISTINCT country
FROM beer-sample
WHERE type = "brewery"
```

Null or missing properties

Throughout our exercises in writing map functions, it was common to test properties before attempting to emit them to a view index. N1QL also provides the capability to check for null or missing properties.

In JavaScript map functions, to check whether a property contains a null value, you simply compare the value to null:

```
if (doc.property == null) // do something
```

Missing properties are not null; rather, they don't exist. In order to check for a missing property with JavaScript, you can compare it to the undefined literal string or simply apply the bang (!) operator to your check. Using the latter test will allow for both a null check and a missing check:

```
if (! doc.property) // do something
```

There are two separate operators in N1QL used to test null and missing property values. The first query in the following snippet tests whether the value for style is Null:

```
SELECT *
FROM beer-sample
WHERE type = "beer"
AND style IS NULL
```

The second tests whether the `style` property was omitted entirely from the beer document:

```
SELECT *
FROM beer-sample
WHERE type = "beer"
AND style IS MISSING
```

These sorts of tests are important, given the schema-less nature of Couchbase and other document databases. Most developers are used to the safety of a relational schema, but in the world of NoSQL, it's important to expect the unexpected!

String utilities

One of the more obvious limitations of querying views is the lack of a proper `LIKE` operator. Though we saw in *Chapter 4, Advanced Views*, that it is possible to emulate a query like "starts with", it is not as robust as SQL's `LIKE` operator.

Fortunately, N1QL addresses this limitation with its own `LIKE` operator. Similar to SQL, you define a search pattern with a wildcard that is specified by a `%` character. In the following snippet, all breweries with Boston in their name will be returned in the results:

```
SELECT *
FROM brewery-sample
WHERE type = "brewery"
AND name LIKE "%Boston%"
```

Other string operators exist to perform standard string transformations such as `SUBSTR`, `LOWER`, `UPPER`, and `LENGTH`. You can use these functions as you do in a JavaScript map function or with string operations in most frameworks:

```
SELECT *
FROM beer-sample
WHERE type = "brewery"
AND LOWER(name) ="thomas hooker brewing"
```

It's also possible to perform string concatenation using the double pipe (||) operator. You can use this operator to combine properties into a single projected property. If you want to combine the city, state, and postal code into a single value, you can write this query:

```
SELECT city || ", " || state || " " || code AS Address
FROM beer-sample
WHERE type = "brewery"
```

```
AND city IS NOT NULL
AND state IS NOT NULL
AND code IS NOT NULL
```

More accurately, in the **beer-sample** bucket, breweries without city, state, or code values are stored as empty strings, so the preceding query won't actually filter the data as you might expect. Instead, you will have check whether those properties have a nonempty string. Which test you perform will of course depend on how your documents are structured:

```
SELECT city || ", " || state || " " || code AS Address
FROM beer-sample
WHERE type = "brewery"
AND city != ""
AND state != ""
AND code != ""
```

Aggregation and math

Performing aggregation is also a familiar operation. To write a query to count the number of breweries by state, you use the built-in count aggregate function:

```
SELECT state, COUNT(*) AS Count
FROM beer-sample
WHERE type = "brewery"
GROUP BY state
```

As you might expect, N1QL supports mathematical and aggregate operations such as AVG, ROUND, MIN, MAX, and SUM. You can use these operations to perform calculations on either aggregated data or on projected columns. As another example of aggregation with N1QL, this query computes the average abv (alcohol by volume) of a brewery's beer brands:

```
SELECT brewery_id, AVG(abv) AS Average
FROM beer-sample
WHERE type = "beer"
AND abv != 0
GROUP BY brewery_id
```

Similarly, if you want to find the beer with the highest or lowest alcohol content, you can use the MAX or MIN function respectively. In the following snippet, the HAVING clause is added to the GROUP BY clause to filter the results:

```
SELECT name, MAX(abv) AS Strength
FROM beer-sample
```

```
WHERE type = "beer"
AND abv != 0
GROUP BY name
HAVING MAX(abv) > 5
```

The BETWEEN operator may also be used to query for documents with a property value within a range; for example, if we want to find beers with abv between 5 and 10, we can use this query:

```
SELECT *
FROM beer-sample
WHERE abv BETWEEN 5 AND 10
```

At the time of writing this book, the BETWEEN operator doesn't work with the AND operator. In order to test for abv and type, you will need to use the "greater than" (>) and "less than" (<) operators:

```
SELECT *
FROM beer-sample
WHERE abv> 5 AND abv< 10
AND type = "beer"
```

Of course, N1QL also supports standard arithmetic operators for multiplication, division, addition, and subtraction. You are able to use these operators in your projections as you could with SQL. The following snippet calculates the proof (twice the abv value) of each beer. Also note the use of the standard "greater than" operator. Of course, the "less than" operator is also supported:

```
SELECT abv * 2 AS proof
FROM beer-sample
WHERE type = "beer"
AND abv> 0
```

> Note that N1QL is smart enough to know when a hyphenated property or bucket name is used in a query, and it won't confuse the query engine into attempting subtraction. There is no need to avoid such properties.

Complex structures

N1QL queries are not limited to simple data types such as strings and numbers. With N1QL, you are able to operate on JSON objects and arrays as you could with map functions written in JavaScript.

As a simple example of a nested object, consider the brewery documents in the **beer-sample** bucket. These documents have geo data contained in a nested object with the geo property:

```
{
  "type": "brewery",
  "geo": {
    "lng": -72.1234,
    "lat": 34.1234
  }
}
```

The geo object contains properties for longitude and latitude. If you want to write a query to find a brewery's geo information, you can use the standard dot (.) notation, which is common with most modern object-oriented programming languages:

```
SELECT geo.lon, geo.lat
FROM beer-sample
WHERE type = "brewery"
```

Arrays are another common data structure in JSON documents. N1QL supports working with arrays in a few ways. The beer-sample database doesn't have much when it comes to interesting array data, but the brewery documents do contain an address property, which is an array. Unfortunately for this example, there is no more than a single address in any brewery document:

```
SELECT address[0]
FROM beer-sample
WHERE type = "brewery"
```

In this case, the result of the query will be the first address (in our case the only address) in each brewery document. N1QL also includes a few functions to work with arrays. If a beer document didn't contain a valid address array, the preceding query would break. A safer query should include a check for the length of the array:

```
SELECT address[0]
FROM beer-sample
WHERE type = "brewery"
AND address[0] IS NOT NULL
AND ARRAY_LENGTH(address[0]) > 0
```

It's also possible to use array slicing to achieve a similar result. The following snippet demonstrates how to select the first two addresses from a brewery document and ensure that those addresses are not missing. Note that the `beer-sample` database doesn't contain address data to satisfy this query:

```
SELECT address[0:2]
FROM beer-sample
WHERE type = "brewery"
AND address[0:2] IS NOT MISSING
```

There are also methods for combining and adding items to arrays, such as `array_prepend`, `array_append`, and `array_concat`. As their names suggest, these methods add elements to the beginning or end of an array, or combine two arrays into one.

Working with collections

N1QL provides a means to succinctly query collections within a document. Recall that to examine nested collections in a map function, you used to run a `for` loop over the items in that collection. To achieve similar results in N1QL queries, you can filter a collection using the `ANY` operator.

For example, if we continue to use the `address` property of brewery documents, we can search for only those addresses that are not empty. In the following example, we're checking the length of each address string as our condition. Note that if a document contained two addresses, where one was valid and another was an empty string, the condition would still be satisfied:

```
SELECT address
FROM beer-sample
WHERE type = "brewery"
AND ANY addr IN address
SATISFIES LENGTH(addr) > 0 END
```

With a very slight change to the query, we can modify the behavior so that instead of returning breweries with a mix of empty and valid addresses in the address array, we return only those documents where all addresses are valid. In this case, we change the `ANY` operator to `EVERY`:

```
SELECT address
FROM beer-sample
WHERE type = "brewery"
AND EVERY addr IN address
SATISFIES LENGTH(addr) > 0 END
```

With EVERY, only documents with address arrays with nonempty entries will be included. This means that if an array contained a valid address (nonempty) and an invalid address (empty), it would be excluded from the results. Note that in the beer-sample database, there aren't any records that do not satisfy the preceding previous query. Again, all address records contain either a single address or an empty array.

Joins

N1QL does contain support to perform joins on documents with a caveat—the joins must be made across different buckets. While this is a limitation for several use cases, it does provide a means of putting data together from disparate document sources.

Since this chapter focuses on the beer-sample database, the following join next imagines a setup where beer and brewery documents are stored in two separate buckets named beers and breweries, respectively:

```
SELECT *
FROM beers AS b
JOIN breweries AS b2
KEYS b.brewery_id
```

SDK support

At the time of writing this book, SDK support for N1QL is somewhat limited. .NET, Java, PHP, and Node.js have experimental support for N1QL. Ruby and Python should see N1QL support in the future. Until both the N1QL framework and the SDKs are more locked down, it's worth keeping an eye out for changes. At this stage, we'll look briefly at a Java snippet that demonstrates how to use N1QL with the 2.0 SDK:

```
Observable<QueryResult> result =
bucket.query("select * from beer-sample");
```

Notice that the N1QL language is reminiscent of working with SQL-oriented frameworks such as JDBC or ADO.NET.

If you're familiar with prepared statements in SQL, where you provide parameters as positional arguments to a query statement with placeholders, there are work items for the Couchbase N1QL team to provide support for these types of queries. The advantage of prepared statements is that the query optimizer doesn't have to reparse and replan the execution with each run of query that differs only by arguments.

Summary

This chapter introduced N1QL, a powerful and experimental Couchbase query language. It's important to understand that this was not an exhaustive introduction to N1QL; some stones were left unturned. In particular, there are several additional functions for working with dates, strings, and numeric values. However, we have seen the most important bits.

As we've seen, N1QL is a somewhat radical departure from the MapReduce view model. This new feature is not meant to replace MapReduce, but rather to create greater flexibility in accessing your data.

Couchbase Server is truly unique because it provides developers with so many options to access data. With three distinct models for accessing documents, developers are able to build applications the way they wish to build them. Some developers will stick to the tried-and-true key/value model, while other developers who enjoy the power of MapReduce are likely to stick to views. Nevertheless, newer Couchbase users who prefer cutting-edge technology will likely find the familiarity of N1QL appealing.

As we'll see in the next chapter, designing a schema for Couchbase means considering both key/value and document design. Adding N1QL to the mix does mean that some of the design considerations made for MapReduce may have to be rethought. However, with N1QL still in developer preview status, we'll consider MapReduce when discussing document schemas.

6
Designing a Schema-less Data Model

In this chapter, we're going to take a step back from how to program for a Couchbase database, and instead focus on design considerations for a Couchbase application. We touched on a few of the important design ideas in the previous chapters, but we'll now explore keys and documents in greater detail.

There is no right way to design a document-based application. This notion differs significantly from relational application design. If you're an experienced developer of RDBMS-based systems, you've likely undergone the process of converting a logical model to a highly normalized database design. NoSQL design is very different.

Proper document design is tightly coupled with both your logical model and your application use cases. Moreover, use-case-based document design will vary among document databases. Designing your Couchbase documents is not necessarily the same as designing your MongoDB documents.

Since Couchbase is a hybrid data store, we'll need to consider both key/value and document designs. Here, our key/value design might differ from a key/value design for a key/value database such as **Redis**. As you explore both key/value and document design, you'll learn about the specifics of Couchbase that impact on design decisions.

Key design

With Couchbase, you can't have a document without a key. Therefore, it's clearly important to have a strategy for key design. How you choose to generate your keys will, generally, be partly preference driven and partly use case driven. We'll start by examining what basic requirements exist for keys in Couchbase.

Keys, metadata, and RAM

We saw previously that Couchbase keys are parts of the metadata of a document. This fact was revealed as we explored views that used the `meta` argument in map functions to retrieve document IDs for indexes. Prior to Couchbase Server 3.0, all keys were kept in the memory even if their documents weren't. Therefore, longer keys required more memory. Since Couchbase performs best when documents are kept in the memory, smaller keys mean more RAM available for documents.

In Couchbase Server 3.0, keeping metadata in the memory is still the default behavior, but it is now tunable. While you're now able to delete metadata from the memory for documents that have been evicted (based on a most recently used strategy), metadata not being in RAM does slow down performance. Hence, the choice of key is still of importance for very large datasets.

Predictable keys

In the relational world, primary keys are almost always autoincremented integers. You generally don't care about that primary key, as you're more likely to access a row in a table by some secondary index. Of course, there are times when you'll display a record by its ID, but it's likely that you found that record's ID via some other lookup, such as a `SELECT *` statement or through a foreign-key-related document.

Couchbase documents are not very different. We're able to get to documents by secondary indexes or even nonconstrained relations. However, these lookups require use of the view API. While Couchbase provides more than satisfactory performance for view lookups, these queries will never be as fast as in-memory document fetches via the key/value API.

If you're designing an application that requires extremely fast performance, avoiding the view API might be desirable. If you need to boost performance via the key/value API, you might want to have predictable keys that your application can use. Creating predictable keys does require some thought, however.

For an example of how we can use predictable keys, let's consider the simple case of a system that pushes messages to a user in a manner similar to that of Twitter or Facebook. Our version will be simplified because we won't concern ourselves with the comparison of read with unread messages. We'll assume that the system regularly updates a view with new messages and refreshes that view during each update.

In such a system, we could start with a user document that has an array of messages:

```
{
  username: "jpage",
  passwordHash: "0123456",
  messages: [
    "Hello!",
    "Great gig!",
  ]
}
```

If we wanted to use a predictable key to find a user's messages, we'd have to use a key that would be accessible via some attributes of the user data; for example, we could use the username as the key. Assuming a user has to log in with their username, the application would be able to provide the key to a key/value Get operation at some interval.

While in this case we would be able to bypass the need for a view to get our user messages, it's not an ideal design. One problem is that if a user changes their username, a new document would have to be created, and keys cannot be renamed! In practice, you could retrieve the original user document, create a copy, and remove the old document. However, this approach does risk leaving an orphaned document behind if the delete operation were to fail.

Another potential problem is that each time the messages are retrieved, the entire document will have to be retrieved. The key/value Get operations do not support projections (selecting subsets of records). As such, it's important to consider document size for the performance of Get. It's always faster to retrieve only the data needed by your application.

While views can be used to provide a part of the document at its messages, remember that this is not good practice. Views should rarely emit document details to be used as it is. Instead, we can use predictable keys to create a simple access pattern to break our documents across multiple keys.

If we break our document into smaller documents with related keys, we could use one of two approaches for using keys. The first approach would be to store the key of the other documents within the parent document; for example, a user document might hold a key reference to a userMessages document.

A second approach would be to use a variant of the predictable parent key for each of the child keys. So, if the parent key were `user::jpage`, then the child keys could be of the `user::profile::jpage` or `user::messages::jpage` form. In this approach, the keys hold some form of taxonomy for the documents, and this can be used to discover the document type within a map function:

```
function(doc, meta) {
  var keyParts = meta.id.split("::");
  if (keyParts[0] == "user") {
    emit(...);
  }
}
```

The preceding approach does have the added benefit of letting you avoid the need to use a `type` property in your documents. This benefit is less about document size (since the key might be larger) and more about not being required to maintain an extra property in your documents.

In practice, including taxonomy in the key is largely a matter of preference. The performance difference during indexing will be nominal, that is, the difference between a string split operation and a string comparison operation. However, smaller keys require less RAM for metadata. If predictability is not important, the `type` property approach does potentially allow for less RAM use.

Unpredictable keys

As you might have surmised, Couchbase Server does not provide a mechanism to generate keys. Therefore, it is up to your application to generate unique keys. There are a couple of different strategies you might employ in creating unique keys, but generally speaking, all you should be concerned with is maintaining uniqueness.

The most common means of generating keys is to use a globally (or universally) unique identifier, typically referred to as a GUID or UUID. Most modern programming platforms support GUID generation. When creating a document, you simply have to create a new GUID and use that value when calling `add` or `set`.

Storing keys

It might seem strange to title a section as *Storing keys*, since you don't actually have a choice as to where keys are stored. However, it's important to note that storing the key inside the document is redundant and potentially invalid if not kept in sync.

The problem of including a key in the document tends to arise when using JSON serializers to create documents from business objects. Consider the following C# class:

```
public class User
{
  public string Id { get; set; }
  public string Username { get; set; }
  public string Email { get; set; }
}
```

What happens when this class is serialized into JSON? Most likely, the Id property will be included in the document. Assuming that you expect this property to map to the key of the document, you'll want to make sure that you ignore this property during serialization. Many JSON serializers provide a means to prevent a property from being serialized. In other cases, you may have to transform the object into an object without an Id property.

On the way out, you will likely want to map the Id property of your domain object to the key of the document. Newer SDKs such as Java and .NET provide this support out of the box. In other cases, you'll simply assign the key used during a Get key/value operation or the key discovered during a view query.

These approaches are illustrated in the following C# snippets. Note that these samples intentionally bypass the built-in JSON support to demonstrate the explicit mapping of Id properties to business objects:

```
public class User
{
  //Don't include this field when serializing
  [JsonIgnore]
  public string Id { get; set; }
  public string Username { get; set; }
  public string Email { get; set; }
}

var key = "12345";
var user = new User
{
  Id = key,
  Username = "jsmith",
  Email = "jsmith@example.com"
};

//Serialize the User instance to JSON
//The Id property will be ignored
```

```
var json = JsonConvert.SerializeObject(user);

//Insert the User JSON
bucket.Insert<string>(user.Id, json);

//Get the JSON string from the bucket
var savedJson = bucket.Get<string>(key);

//Deserialize the JSON back into a User instance
var savedUser = JsonConvert.DeserializeObject<User>(savedJson);

//The savedUser will have a null Id at this point
//Manually set the Id property to the key
savedUser.Id = key
```

From this example, you might be wondering why you need to set the Id property of the savedUser instance to a key when you already know the key. The assumption here is that your application will somehow make use of this data object and attempt to access the Id value. Suppose you were making use of this object in an HTML templating engine. You could display an **Edit User** link using this code:

```
<a href="/Edit/@user.Id">Edit User</a>
```

Key restrictions

Regardless of which key strategy you choose, there are a couple of minor restrictions on keys; for example, they are strings no more than 250 bytes long. Also, you cannot use spaces in your keys, but as we saw in the previous case, you may use characters such as punctuation to delimit a key.

Document design

Document design is a more involved activity than key design. There are far more variables to consider when creating a document's schema. Some of these factors are specific to Couchbase. Others are generally applicable to document databases.

Denormalization

When designing a relational system, you typically start with a highly denormalized logical view of your entities. That view is then normalized into a physical model where the data is spread across several tables in an effort to minimize any possible data redundancy.

Similarly, you'll likely start your document design by creating a denormalized, logical model. With this approach, your design first considers the most complete document that your domain demands. For example, if you were building a blog, you might start with a blog document with nested posts. Within each post, there would be nested comments and tags:

```
{
    "type": "blog",
    "title": "John Zablocki'sdllHell.net",
    "author": {
        "name": "john.zablocki",
        "email": "jz@example.com"
    },
    "posts": [
    {
        "title": "Couchbase Schema Design",
        "body": [
            "Couchbase schema design..."
        ],
        "date": "2015-01-05",
        "tags": [
            "couchbase",
            "nosql",
            "schema"
        ],
        "comments": [
            {
                "comment": "Thanks for the post.",
                "user": "jsmith"
            }
        ]
    },
    {
        "title": "Azure DocumentDB",
        "body": [
            "Using Azure DocumentDB..."
        ],
        "tags": [
            "azure",
            "nosql"
        ],
        "comments": [
            {
                "comment": "Thanks for the post.",
                "user": "jsmith"
            },
            {
```

```
        "comment": "Interesting.",
          "user": "jdoe"
      }
    ]
  }
  ]
}
```

Next, you'll create a physical model with a goal of minimizing normalization. In other words, you'll design a schema where related entities are broken apart only when necessary.

In the previous blog example, the normalized relational model would likely include separate tables for blogs, posts, comments, and tags. The process of creating a minimally normalized document model should follow from considering use cases for your application.

A good way to start in the case of a blog is to separate posts from the parent blog. This step of normalization is important because without it, every time a blog post is read, the blog, the post, and all sibling posts will be retrieved as well. Clearly, it's best to be able to retrieve a single blog post:

```
//key blog_johnzablockis_dllhellnet
{
  "type": "blog",
  "title": "John Zablocki'sdllHell.net",
  "author": "author": {
    "name": "john.zablocki",
    "email": "jz@example.com"
  }
}

//key post_couchbase_schema_design
{
  "blogId": "johnzablockis_dllhellnet",
  "title": "Couchbase Schema Design",
  "body": [
    "Couchbase schema design..."
  ],
  "date": "2015-01-05",
  "tags": [
    "couchbase",
    "nosql",
    "schema"
  ],
  "comments": [
    {
```

```
        "comment": "Thanks for the post.",
        "user": "jsmith"
      }
    ]
  }
```

The separate blog and post documents here demonstrate how to link two documents together by placing the key of one document on the related document. In this case, we have the blog document's key on the post document in its `blogId` property.

If we assume that each blog has only one author, we have another decision to make—where to put the author details. One option is to separate the authors into their own documents. If we were to take this approach, then in order to show an author's name on a post, we'd either have to get to the author document through the blog document, or include a second ID reference on posts, which would be the author document's key.

Alternatively, there is a valid approach that involves keeping the author details within the blog, and (redundantly) including the name of the author in the post document. With this approach, we avoid the need to retrieve additional documents to simply add a name for display:

```
{
  "blogId": "johnzablockis_dllhellnet",
  "title": "Couchbase Schema Design",
  "author": "john.zablocki",
  "body": [
    "Couchbase schema design..."
  ]
}
```

 If you're a relational developer, this last step probably feels a bit "dirty." That's common at first when moving to NoSQL. Remember that NoSQL databases exist to make programming against databases easier and to provide optimal performance. Denormalizing data by being redundant is a tool to achieve both of these goals. Moreover, you are likely to optimize your relational model by denormalizing a column or two to avoid an extra join or query. However, this approach does of course require some maintenance effort to ensure data integrity.

The decision as to whether to leave comments within posts will be discussed later in this chapter, as it is a more nuanced choice to make, compared to blogs and posts. As for tags, it would be very inefficient to normalize tags into their own documents as you might do with a relational system; each tag would require a `Get` operation.

One reason the normalized model works so well in relational systems is that SQL joins allow related data to be gathered from several different tables and presented as a single logical result. However, joins also create overhead for queries by increasing disk access operations.

Most NoSQL systems have forgone join support and rely heavily on the cache to support rapid retrieval of several documents when a somewhat normalized document is required. Couchbase is capable of tens of thousands of operations per second on a single node. As such, multi-get overhead is generally not a concern.

Object-to-document mappings

When you design an application, you tend to model your business or domain objects much more closely with your logical model than your physical model. This conflict leads to what is often termed as the **object-relational impedance mismatch**, which is another way of saying that it's hard to map your domain objects to your relational model.

With document stores, you have a much easier path from the object to the document. For starters, JSON (and its binary variant) is itself a notation for describing objects. Within a document, there is built-in support for nested collections, related properties, and basic property types. More importantly, pretty much all modern programming languages have JSON serializers.

It won't always make sense to store the entirety of a domain object graph in a single document, but as a general rule, it's useful to start with this design and to allow your use cases to dictate document separation.

Data types

With relational databases, there are numerous types that may be used to create a schema. From fixed-length to variable-length strings and floating-point numbers with various precisions, SQL systems support a great number of options. The situation is quite different with Couchbase Server.

As a document store relying heavily on JSON, Couchbase needs only a few primitive types supported by JSON. These types are strings, numbers, arrays, and Booleans. From these types, virtually any object graph can be stored as a document. Note that dates are not addressed by the JSON standard.

Document separation

There is no golden rule as to when you should separate your document into smaller documents. We saw earlier in this chapter that performance considerations might lead us to do so, but there are also a few other reasons that don't necessarily involve speed of document retrieval.

One common reason for breaking a document into smaller documents is write contention. Consider a blog post and its comments. In the following abbreviated document, we can see that each comment on a post is stored as a nested object within a comments collection. While this is certainly a valid document design, there are situations where it might not be optimal:

```
{
    "title": "Couchbase Schema Design",
    "body": "Designing documents...",
    "type": "post",
    "comments": [
        { "message": "Great post", "user": "rplant" },
        { "message": "I learned a lot", "user": "jpjones" },
    ]
}
```

Consider a situation where a blog post is quite popular and is likely to generate hundreds (or even thousands) of comments in a short period of time. In this case, it is important to understand one aspect of Couchbase document retrieval, that it's all or nothing.

When you perform a Get operation on a document, the entire document is returned. While Couchbase is quite fast and that document is likely coming from the RAM (not the disk), it still means every page view would pull back all comments. If you're not displaying those comments, then you're retrieving a potentially significant amount of data for no reason.

While you may not be concerned with the transfer of unused data when the document is retrieved, there is another consideration for such a document design. If hundreds or thousands of users are trying to update a document at the same time, there will be contention for that document. Using CAS for optimistic locking is certainly a requirement here, but CAS will only prevent stale updates, it won't minimize contention.

As an alternative, you could separate each comment into its own small document. In doing so, you eliminate the need to perform CAS operations and keep the post document lean:

```
{
    "message": "Great post",
    "user": "rplant" ,
    "type": "comment",
    "postId": "couchbase_schema_design"
}
```

To find all comments associated with a given post, you can create a view where the index is on the postId property of the comment document:

```
function(doc, meta) {
    if (doc.type == "comment" && doc.postId) {
        emit(doc.postId);
    }
}
```

Again, whether this approach makes sense for your situation depends primarily on the needs of your particular application. If a post document were to get only a dozen or so comments, there is little need to worry about CAS impacting performance. There would also be little concern over document size and retrieving superfluous data.

 Keep in mind that with the approach of breaking nested entities into separate documents, you're increasing the RAM requirements for metadata. Having a single document means having only one key and associated metadata values.

Another reason you might consider breaking a document into separate documents is about document access patterns. Recall that Couchbase Server keeps recently used documents in the memory whenever possible. Storing related data together in a single document means potentially storing unnecessary data in the RAM.

As an example of how to design for this scenario, consider an activity where you track customers and customer orders. The denormalized approach would be to have a customer document with a nested collection of orders:

```
{
    "username": "tyorke",
    "type": "customer",
    "orders": [
        { "description": "microphone": "date": "2014-11-02" },
```

```
    { "description": "drum machine": "date": "2014-11-02" }
  ]
}
```

The problem with this document design is that a customer is likely to spend more time visiting an online store than actually creating orders. If the RAM is a constraint for your cluster, you should consider separating the order documents into a separate document. That way, the less frequently used order details are less likely to occupy the RAM when resources are constrained:

```
{
  "type": "customerOrders",
  "customerId": "tyorke",
  "orders": [
    { "description": "microphone": "date": "2014-11-02" },
    { "description": "drum machine": "date": "2014-11-02" }
  ]
}
```

It should be clear from our brief discussion of document separation that the saying "no single size fits all" holds true here. Your application, more than well-defined academic rules, will dictate how to segment your documents.

Finally, it's worth noting that documents in Couchbase are limited to 20 megabytes in size. While in practice, this limitation is rarely an issue, it should be kept in mind if you decide to store binary data or other large structures. If you reach this limit, you might be forced to separate your documents regardless of the considerations discussed previously.

Object schemas

Although schema-less databases such as Couchbase don't impose any structure on your documents, it's likely that your application will. We've already discussed the advantages of document databases in terms of natural object mapping. Another benefit of this mapping is that your application effective defines the schema for documents in your Couchbase buckets.

Allowing your datastore to be given a schema from the application layer is not unique to document databases. Over the past decade or so, it has become common to use ORM libraries with **code-first** database design. With this approach, you create a domain object and allow a certain tool to create your database schema from these objects.

In the .NET world, the **entity framework** will allow you to define classes in C# and then generate a database from those entities. The tables will match the class names, and the columns will match the types and names of the properties. In Ruby, an **active record** allows database schemas to be created from Ruby classes. Other frameworks have similar libraries.

Code-first tends to be implicit with document databases. Since each document you create was likely the result of serializing an object into JSON, that object defined the schema for the resultant document.

There are some caveats to allowing your objects to become your document schemas. Earlier in this chapter, we saw the problem of serializing an Id property into a document. You may also want to exclude other properties from being serialized.

If we consider the brewery and beer documents from the **beer-sample** bucket, we'd have a Beer class in our application that has a property referencing its brewery. This property would exist primarily for the purpose of navigation between related objects:

```
public class Beer
{
    public string Id { get; set; }
    public string Name { get; set; }
    public string Type { get; set; }
    public string BreweryId { get; set; }
    public Brewery Brewery { get; set; }
}
```

If we serialized the preceding C# class, we'd end up with a nested brewery. As we know, however, these documents are separated in the brewery-sample database. To avoid this problem, you'll need to instruct your JSON serializer to ignore certain properties. In .NET, the JSON.NET library supports attributes for this purpose:

```
public class Beer
{
    [JsonIgnore]
    public string Id { get; set; }
    public string Name { get; set; }
    public string Type { get; set; }
    public string BreweryId { get; set; }
    [JsonIgnore]
    public Brewery Brewery { get; set; }
}
```

Schema-less structure changes

An important consideration when allowing your objects to create your document schemas is versioning. A big advantage of schema-less databases is that your data model is free to change without having to deal with relational-style schema changes. For example, dropping or adding a column might lock a table or require downtime for your SQL-database-backed application.

Because there is the flexibility of having no database-imposed schema, it does not mean you are free from schema change concerns. If you are using object-to-document mappings, you've effectively created a strongly typed document database. If your object changes, it may no longer match its document, and vice versa.

It's likely that your platform's JSON serializer that will determine the impact of schema changes. If your document has a property that's no longer applicable to your object, deserialization could cause a runtime error. Similarly, serializing a changed object could create variations in documents of the same type, creating unintended view results.

One approach to addressing this problem is to add a version number property to your documents. With this approach, your application and your views may react differently to changes based on the version of the document being read or written.

Another approach is to validate and/or modify document schemas before making any application layer changes. It is possible to write a view to find all the unique document schemas in your bucket:

```
function (doc, meta) {
  if (doc.type) {
    var props = [];
    for (var prop in doc) {
      props.push(prop);
    }
    emit({ "type" : doc.type, "schema" : props.sort() });
  }
}
```

In the preceding map function, we first check whether the document has a type property. This step is not required, but we assume that any document in the bucket related to an object has a type property associated with it. After this step, each of the properties of the document is pushed into an array.

The keys of this index are JSON objects that include the document type and the sorted set of properties from the document:

```json
{
  "id": "becca",
  "key": {
    "type": "user",
    "schema": [
      "email",
      "firstName",
      "lastName",
      "type"
    ]
  },
  "value": null
}, {
  "id": "hank",
  "key": {
    "type": "user",
    "schema": [
      "firstName",
      "lastName",
      "type"
    ]
  },
  "value": null
}, {
  "id": "karen",
  "key": {
    "type": "user",
    "schema": [
      "firstName",
      "lastName",
      "type"
    ]
  },
  "value": null
}
```

In its current state, this view is not completely useful. However, if you add a reduce function with the built-in `_count` function, and group the results by setting the **group** option to `true`, then you will get a list of all unique schemas and a count of documents with those schemas:

```json
{
  "key": {
    "type": "user",
```

```
        "schema": [
          "email",
          "firstName",
          "lastName",
          "type"
        ]
    },
    "value": 1
  },
  {
    "key": {
      "type": "user",
      "schema": [
        "firstName",
        "lastName",
        "type"
      ]
    },
    "value": 2
}
```

You can also easily write a view to locate documents with or without a particular property. If you want to find all user documents without an `email` property, you can use the following map function:

```
function(doc, meta) {
  if (doc.type == "user" && ! doc.email) {
    emit(null, null);
  }
}
```

These views demonstrate how to find information about document schemas. With this information, you can iterate over the results and update documents to have an updated schema.

 If you're willing to lose the benefits of user-defined types, you should consider using dictionary structures in your application. Dictionaries map naturally to JSON and have less risk of breaking on schema mismatches.

Object and document properties

Another advantage of having document schemas derived from classes is that your documents will inherit name and data types from your objects. Generally speaking, this behavior should be acceptable. However, there are a couple of issues we need to be aware of.

Perhaps, the most important consideration here is about document property names. JSON became popular for data transfer in part due to its relative terseness when compared to XML. However, with no database-defined schema, Couchbase documents repeatedly include the same schema information across potentially billions of documents.

Long names take up more RAM and more disk space. While this is not an issue for smaller apps, large datasets may need to be optimized to have smaller property names. Fortunately, most JSON serializers support property name mapping. For example, in .NET a user class could be mapped as follows:

```
public class User
{
  [JsonProperty("fn")]
  public string FirstName { get; set; }
  [JsonProperty("ln")]
  public string LastName { get; set; }
  [JsonProperty("t")]
  public string Type { get; set; }
}
```

When this class is serialized, it will be a smaller document that has the properties mapped and unchanged:

```
{
  "fn": "Wolfgang",
  "ln": "Mozart",
  "t": "user"
}
```

It's also important to understand how your JSON serializer maps property types. While strings and numbers will be consistent, dates may not be consistent. Make sure you check your platform's JSON serialization behavior.

Document relationships

Another important design consideration is about dealing with document relationships. Throughout this chapter, we saw how to separate related documents but we haven't fully discussed how to work with related documents.

With document databases, the basic approach to handling relationships involves including the ID of a related document with the relating document. We've seen this design in the previous blog sample and in the `beer-sample` database, where beer documents include a `brewery_id` property. Again, this is a convention and there is no database constraint.

Without database-enforced referential integrity, your application layer will be responsible for enforcing data validity. Once again, views may be used to identify where deficiencies in data exist. For example, if we want to find all beer names whose brewery ID is invalid, we can simply iterate over the results of the collated view example in *Chapter 4*, *Advanced Views*, looking for beer names without a matching brewery.

One of the advantages of relational constraints and joins is that your object-relational mapper is able to assemble your object graph for your application. Without formal relationships in Couchbase (or other document databases), your application will have to perform multiple queries to get related documents, and manually assemble your object graph.

Finalizing the schema

When designing relational systems, you often end up with some data being denormalized for performance or other reasons. As joins prove costly, a typical optimization step is to create flattened tables, where redundant columns are close to the data to which they're related.

With document databases, you'll likely end where you started, with a mostly denormalized document structure. Not only does a denormalized document store related data together, it also is likely to include properties from other documents that are not primary keys.

As an example of a denormalized relationship, consider the blog post and comment example. If comments are to be displayed with their respective authors, then either numerous lookups must be made to user documents, or some subset of author details must be stored redundantly with each comment.

As with relationships based on IDs, other properties might change in their primary location, forcing your application to know how to update the redundant records. If a user changes their username, not only user documents but also all comments by that user will need to be updated.

Summary

As we saw in this chapter, designing Couchbase documents is partly art and partly science. More than relational systems and most other NoSQL systems, Couchbase's schema-less design requires great care, not just because Couchbase is a hybrid key/ value and document store system.

Many developers choose Couchbase for its performance. Designing a document-based system for scaling involves a unique set of constraints and concerns. Other developers choose Couchbase for its flexibility. Designing a document-based system for flexibility raises several unique considerations for applications.

Those developers who choose Couchbase for both its flexibility and its scalability have the added challenge of trying to tweak performance without sacrificing the flexibility of a document database.

It's always tempting to approach system design by sticking to what we know. It's important to remember that Couchbase is a truly unique system, and your document design will not necessarily seem obvious at first. However, you shouldn't be afraid to allow some parts of your design to feel relational and others to feel nonrelational.

In the next chapter, we're going to continue to explore application designs in a schema-less world. While creating a simple, Couchbase-based web application, we'll be able to work through several issues we explored in this chapter.

7

Creating a To-do App with Couchbase

In this chapter, we'll put together everything you learned so far. In recent years, the to-do app has replaced the blog as the canonical first app when learning a new platform. While a to-do app seems simple on the surface, it is complex enough to demonstrate most of the core features of a framework.

A to-do app built on Couchbase is well suited to demonstrate both the key/value and document features of Couchbase. With some minor feature additions to a typical to-do app, we'll be able to make use of some of the advanced view features available for Couchbase developers.

Throughout this chapter, we'll focus more on general design considerations rather than specific SDK or language constructs. As was the case in the previous chapters, we'll explore multiple SDKs as we build our to-do app. While the basic language constructs may vary from SDK to SDK, the broad strokes approach will not vary.

A simple to-do schema

You've learned in previous chapters that schema design in the world of schema-less NoSQL databases tends to derive from the logical or object design of the application layer. As such, we'll start our application development efforts by considering the design of the classes we'll use in our application.

In the simplest case, a to-do app is nothing more than a checklist. To start modeling our schema, we'll limit the design to two properties of a checklist, namely a description and a checkbox. This design is shown in the following C# class:

```
public class Task
{
  public string Description { get; set; }
  public bool IsComplete { get; set; }
}
```

In this class, the `Description` property describes the task to be done. The Boolean property `IsComplete` simply checks whether the task has been completed. The corresponding JSON document stored in Couchbase mirrors this class:

```
{
  "description": "Pick up the almond milk",
  "isComplete": false
}
```

As we build our application, we'll add more features and develop our schema further. For now however, we'll start building the application to support our simple task list.

Working with SDKs

Again, it's not feasible within the scope of a single chapter to implement an application with a single framework that would satisfy all readers. Even a cross-platform language such as Python would require a rather lengthy exploration into setting up a development environment and exploring a web framework and its components.

Java and .NET are quite popular platforms, but require a fair bit of tooling support to get these platforms up and running. Focusing exclusively on one of these platforms would almost certainly alienate a significant number of readers. And, of course, there are differences across Windows, Linux, and Mac OS X.

Instead, we'll focus on the general principles and patterns of Couchbase SDK development. We'll explore constructs that will be broadly applicable to developing a Couchbase application, regardless of your development environment.

Also, we won't dig into any particular web framework but will discuss general web development patterns. Chances are that if you're a web developer and you're working with a NoSQL database, you're likely using a framework that supports capabilities like **MVC** (short for **model-view-controller**).

A brief overview of MVC

For the purpose of this chapter, all you'll need to know of MVC or a similarly-patterned web framework is that when you navigate to a URI such as `http://localhost/tasks/list`, you will have a corresponding server-side method that handles the request to the `list` action. Similarly, a request to `http://localhost/tasks/create` would have a corresponding `create` action. Actions are simply methods invoked on the server that handle an HTTP request and return an HTTP response.

For example, using the popular ASP.NET MVC framework, if you wanted to show a form to create a task when a user navigated to `http://localhost/tasks/create`, you would create a controller named `tasks` and a method (or action) named `create`:

```
public class TasksController : Controller
{
  [HttpGet]
  public ActionResult Create()
  {
    return View();
  }
}
```

As is common with MVC, you create a `Controller` class where the name of the controller reflects some portion of the requested URI path (`tasks` in this case). Within that controller, you define a method, and that method is also reflected in the path (`create` in this case). The previous ASP.NET MVC snippet shows a `create` action that will handle only `HttpGet` requests.

Similarly, to handle the postback data from the HTML form to the server, you create an action to handle the form submission. In ASP.NET MVC, this is done by placing an `HttpPost` attribute on a method matching the name of the action:

```
[HttpPost]
public ActionResult Create(FormCollection form)
{
  //do something with the form
  return RedirectToAction("List");
}
```

Most MVC frameworks follow a similar convention. MVC frameworks such as Ruby's Rails vary slightly in how they handle the different HTTP verbs presented to an action:

```
class TasksController<ApplicationController

  def new
```

```
    end

    def create
      #do something
      redirect_to :action => "Index"
    end
  end
```

In this Rails snippet, we see a similar convention as used by MVC, the primary difference being that the ASP.NET MVC uses attributes to distinguish between GET and POST actions. Other frameworks have a single method that checks the verb to decide how to perform operations.

A variation of popular MVC frameworks is a so-called **micro framework**. Generally speaking, you could think of a web micro framework as an MVC framework without the "C" (that is, the controller). With such frameworks, you'll typically define the path handled by an action, without a controller involved.

A popular micro framework in the Python world is **Flask**. With Flask, you set up a series of routes and instruct Flask on how to dispatch requests to the appropriate handlers. For example, to handle the simple rendering of a create view, the following flask snippet would be used:

```
@app.route("/tasks/create")
def create():
  return render_view("create.html")
```

That same method can be expanded to handle the post back of data, as follows:

```
@app.route("/tasks/create")
def create():
  if request.method == "POST":
    #do something
    return redirect(url_for("index"))
  return render_view("create.html")
```

If you are already familiar with a web framework, the preceding samples should seem familiar. If you have not used a web framework, then you will see snippets like these throughout the remainder of this chapter. For our purpose, it's most important that you have a basic understanding of what these action methods are doing, rather than detailed knowledge of a particular framework.

Using SDK clients

In *Chapter 2, Using Couchbase CRUD Operations*, we explored the basics of obtaining SDK client libraries. Generally, this was achieved via your platform's package manager (for example, NuGet, Gems, or PIP). Assuming that you've obtained your platform's SDK, the first thing you'll need to understand is how to configure and instantiate that client.

Regardless of which SDK you are using, each SDK requires the same basic setup configuration — the location of a node in your cluster and the bucket with which you want to connect. The Python SDK demonstrates this process succinctly:

```
from couchbase import Couchbase
client = Couchbase.connect(host = "localhost", bucket = "beer-
sample")
```

When a Couchbase SDK connects to a node in your cluster, it begins listening to a streaming (over HTTP) message from the server. The content sent through this stream provides the SDK with information on the topology of the cluster, such as how many nodes are active in the cluster and where keys should be sent to or requested from.

This handshake is relatively expensive, and therefore it is generally best practice not to create a client instance except when necessary. Within the scope of a web application, you'd want to have a single client handle all requests, typically by creating a static or shared instance of your client.

In the preceding Python snippet, the `connect` method is provided with limited details about the cluster. Also, in the Python snippet there are a few default values (such as ports) being used by the client. Similarly, the .NET 2.0 SDK may be configured with all defaults that connect to your `localhost` and default bucket:

```
private static Cluster _cluster = new Cluster();
var bucket = _cluster.OpenBucket();
```

The story is similar for other SDKs. You'll create a client by connecting to the cluster and then a bucket. If you're wondering which node in a cluster should be provided in the initial connection, the short answer is *any*. However, it is better to provide multiple nodes in case the node you specified undergoes failover.

The SDKs offer a means of providing multiple URIs via either a configuration file or parameters to connection methods. For example, in Java you could provide multiple URIs to the `create` factory method of the `CouchbaseCluster` class:

```
Cluster cluster = new CouchbaseCluster.create("192.168.0.1",
"192.168.0.2");
```

In this example, if the first URI is not accessible, the SDK would then try to obtain information about cluster configuration from the second URI. How many nodes you should specify depends on your cluster, but generally, at least two and up to three or four nodes should be reasonable.

Creating a task

At this point, we've designed a very simple to-do schema where our tasks are simply checklist items. Regardless of which web framework you are using, you'll need some sort of HTML form to collect the description and isComplete properties of the new tasks:

```html
<html>
  <head>
    <title>Create a Task</title>
  </head>
  <body>
    <form action="tasks/create" method="POST">
      <div>Description:
        <input type="text" name="description" />
      </div>
      <div>Complete:
        <input type="checkbox" name="isComplete" />
      </div>
      </div><button type="submit" value="Save" />
    </form>
  </body>
</html>
```

The preceding HTML form collects these two properties and submits them to a server-side action named create. As an example of how you can respond to this form post, consider the following Python Flask snippet:

```python
@app.route("/tasks/create", methods=["GET","POST"])
def create():
  if request.method == "POST":

    task = { "description": request.form["description"],
      "isComplete": request.form["isComplete"] }
    key = uuid.uuid1().hex
    doc = json.dumps(task)
    client.set(key, doc)
    return redirect(url_for("index"))
  return render_view("create.html")
```

We can see the basic pattern of creating new documents with Couchbase in the preceding lines. These steps are similar to those you'd perform when working with a relational database, but there are a couple of differences.

In this example, the task is constructed as a Python dictionary instance. Alternatively, we could have used a class with properties matching the task fields. Because there is no obvious property of the task to use as a key, a UUID is generated and used as the key for the document. Finally, before saving the task to Couchbase, it is serialized to a JSON document using Python's JSON module.

These last two steps are the primary difference between Couchbase and other databases. Couchbase Server doesn't provide a means to generate keys, so we need to generate our own. Couchbase clients don't enforce JSON as a serialization format, so we need to take care of this ourselves.

Listing tasks

In the preceding snippet, after the task is created, a redirect to an index page is performed. This page is a list page used to view tasks. Building a list page requires finding all our tasks that will require a slight change to our model:

```
public class Task
{
  public string Description { get; set; }
  public bool IsComplete { get; set; }
  public bool Type { get { return "task"; }
}
```

Recall our discussion from the previous chapters on the use of a `type` property on documents to provide a classification for related documents, much in the way a table does for relational databases. In our to-do application, to identify tasks, we'll add a `type` property (which is read-only). The property is set to the `task` string, which will ensure that all task documents are serialized with this type. With this addition, we're ready to write our list page, starting with a map function:

```
//view named "all" in a design doc "tasks"
function(doc, meta) {
  if (doc.type == "task") {
    emit(null, null);
  }
}
```

Notice that this map function doesn't explicitly index any properties of task documents. Since we are indexing only documents marked as tasks, a query on this view will return only the documents we wish to list on our index page. The following C# example is intentionally verbose to illustrate a couple of points. Note that the .NET 1.3 SDK provides some helper methods to achieve similar behavior:

```
public ActionResult Index()
{
  var view = client.GetView<Task>("all"", "tasks");
  var model = GetTasksFromView(view);
  return View(model);
}

private IEnumerable<Task>GetTasksFromView(IView view) {
  foreach(var row in view)
  {
    var doc = client.Get<string>(row.ItemId);
    yield return JsonConvert.DeserializeObject<Task>(doc);
  }
}
```

The `Index` action starts by querying the `all` view in the `tasks` design document. Once the index of the results has been returned, the view is converted to an enumerable list of `Task` instances. In C#, yield return allows a function to be treated as an enumerable object, which means that the casting of a view row to a `Task` instance occurs only when the caller enumerates the results. In this case, the client is an ASP.NET MVC Razor view:

```
<table>
  <thead>
    <tr>
      <th>Description</th>
      <th>Complete</th>
    </tr>
  </thead>
  @foreach(var item in Model)
  {
    <tr>
      <td>@item.Description</td>
      <td>@item.IsComplete</td>
    </tr>
  }
</table>
```

Regardless of which web framework you work with, the basic idea will be the same. You'll query a view, get the results, and pass those results to a view to be displayed. Once this list is complete, the next logical step is to allow the editing of tasks. This action will be similar to the `create` task we've worked on before.

To allow editing, we'll need to allow users to get to the `edit` page for a specific task. This requirement will necessitate adding a property to our class to map to the document's key. This change is important because we must be careful how to map our key, ensuring that JSON serializers don't include a store inside the document:

```
public class Task
{
  [JsonIgnore]
  public string Id { get; set; }

  //other properties omitted
}
```

How you exclude the `Id` property from being serialized into the stored Couchbase document will of course vary by your language and its preferred serializer. In this snippet, an attribute is included on the `Id` property to instruct the JSON.NET serializer to ignore this property.

Although you're ignoring the `Id` property as the document is sent to Couchbase, it's important to remember that you'll want to set it to come out of the bucket. We'll see how to do this by modifying the preceding method that retrieves all task documents for listing:

```
private IEnumerable<Task>GetTasksFromView(IView view) {
  foreach(var row in view)
  {
    var doc = client.Get<string>(row.ItemId);

    //this line will populate all task properties,
//except for Id
    var task  = JsonConvert.DeserializeObject<Task>(doc);

    //explicitly map the document's key to the
    //Id property of the Task instance
    task.Id = row.ItemId;
  }
}
```

We'll also want to modify our list's view code so that we can create a link to the `edit` action we're about to build. In this case, we're simply wrapping the task's `description` column with a link to the `edit` page, with the item's `id` property passed as a parameter to the request. If you're using Flask with its default **Jinja2** templating engine, the list would look like this:

```
{% for item in model %}
  <tr>
    <td><a href="/tasks/edit/{{item.id }}">
      {{ item.description }}</a>
    <td>{{ item.is_complete }}</td>
  </tr>
{% endfor %}
```

The `edit` method on the server will look a bit like the `create` method, except that it will modify the saved document on submission and return the unchanged saved document when the form is displayed:

```
@app.route("/tasks/edit/<key>", methods=["GET","POST"])
def edit(key):

  saved_doc = client.get(key) #retrieve from the bucket

  #deserializesaved_doc to a Task class instance
  saved_task = json.loads(saved_doc)
  saved_task.id = key #manually map the key to the id

  if request.method == "POST":

    #update the editable fields
    saved_task.description = request.form["description"]
    saved_task.is_complete = request.form["is_complete"]

    json_doc = json.dumps(task)
    client.set(key, json_doc)
    return redirect(url_for("index"))
  return render_view("edit.html",  model=saved_task)
```

Regardless of which language or client you are using, the basic pattern will be the same for all editing scenarios. You start by getting the `id` parameter from the request, and use that parameter to look up the saved document via the key/value `get` operation. Then you convert the JSON document to an instance of a `Task` class.

If you are showing the form to edit the task (an HTTP GET request), then you'll pass that task to the form so that it can be rendered with prefilled data. The following Flask Jinja2 template demonstrates how this process works:

```
<form action="/tasks/edit" method="POST">
  <div>Description:
    <input type="text" name="description" value="{{ model.description
}}" />
  </div>
  <div>Complete:
    <input type="checkbox" name="isComplete"  {{ 'checked="checked"'
if model.is_complete }}/>
  </div>
  <div>
    <input type="hidden" name="id" value="{{ model.id }}" />
    <button type="submit" value="Save" />
  </div>
</form>
```

To round out our CRUD task list, we need to include an option to delete tasks. We'll keep this feature simple and leave the "Are you sure you want to delete this item?" alert that typically precedes such an action. We'll start by rearranging the table that displays our task list so that an **Edit** and a **Delete** link appear to the right of each task:

```
{% for item in model %}
  <tr>
    <td>{{ item.description }}</td>
    <td>{{ item.is_complete }}</td>
    <td>
      <a href="/tasks/Edit/{{ item.id }}>Edit</a>
      <a href="/tasks/delete/{{ item.id }}">Delete</a>
  </tr>
{% endfor %}
```

When a user clicks on **Delete**, the delete action will be called on the server, which will get the id property from the query string and then remove the item using the key/value API:

```
@app.route("/tasks/delete/<key>", methods=["GET"])
def delete(key):

    client.delete(key)

    return redirect(url_for("index"))
```

Again, you'd typically not delete an item so freely over an HTTP GET request. The important point here is to understand that when you remove an item, it is always deleted by its key. There is no Couchbase equivalent of SQL's DELETE FROM Table WHERE Column = 'VALUE' statement. If you need to remove an item based on another value, you'll have to create a view to find that value's key and then remove it.

Showing only incomplete tasks

If we want to include a list view that displays only tasks that are not yet marked as complete, we'll need to modify our view to incorporate this change. The following snippet shows this modification. The action and view for the corresponding list page differ only in the name of the Couchbase view queried by the client (for example, all_incomplete and all):

```
//view named "all_incomplete" in the "tasks" design document
function(doc, meta) {
  if (doc.type == "task" && doc.isComplete === false) {
    emit(null, null);
  }
}
```

Notice that the check for incomplete status explicitly uses JavaScript's === operator. If you haven't used this operator, you should now know that it performs an explicit type check along with a value check. The reason to use it here is that ! doc. isComplete would return false if the property is undefined (which might be acceptable in this particular case, but not in most other cases).

Alternatively, we can create a view where the isComplete property is indexed, allowing us to list complete, incomplete, or all tasks. To do so, we'll simply emit the isComplete property instead of null for the view's key:

```
function(doc, meta) {
  if (doc.type == "task") {
    emit(doc.isComplete, null);
  }
}
```

When the query is made to the task list, the desired complete status is either included or omitted entirely:

```
#find all complete
client.query("tasks", "by_status", key=true)

#find all incomplete
```

```
client.query("tasks", "by_status", key=false)

#find all
client.query("tasks", "by_status")
```

Nested tasks

To make our simple task list app a little more interesting, we'll add the ability to nest tasks. In other words, we'll allow some tasks to be subtasks of other tasks. Doing so requires only a slight change to our model, for example adding a `ParentId` property:

```
public class Task
{
  public string Description { get; set; }
  public bool IsComplete { get; set; }
  public string ParentId { get; set; }
  public bool Type { get { return "task"; } }
}
```

There are numerous ways to set up a user interface to allow parent tasks to be set. In the interest of brevity, we'll assume that our `create` and `edit` actions and views have two simple additions:

```
#get all tasks returned by the
#all_incomplete view in the tasks design document
tasks = client.query("tasks", "all_incomplete")

#when saving tasks, assign the parentId
task.parent_id = request.form["parentId"]

#pass the tasks to the view
#model passed only for edit
return render_template("index.html", model=task, tasks=tasks)

<!-- parent task field in HTML form -->
<select name="parentId">
  {% for task in tasks %}
  <option value="task.id">task.Description</option>
  {% endfor %}
</select>
```

The preceding snippet demonstrates that we'll need to query for all incomplete tasks, pass those tasks to the view for use as the data in an HTML `select` element, and assign the selected value back to the task we save on posting the data back.

To view tasks and their children, we'll need to write a view that groups related documents. The approach we'll use will be similar to the example in *Chapter 5, Introducing N1QL*, where we created a collated view to show breweries and their beer types. The only real difference here is that we have a single type of document with a reference to itself:

```
function(doc, meta) {
    if (doc.type == "task") {
        if (! doc.parentId || (doc.parentId == "")) {
            emit([meta.Id, 0], null);
        } else {
            emit([doc.parentId, 1], null);
        }
    }
}
```

In the preceding map function, we first perform the standard type check. Next, we check whether a document has a parentId property. If it does, we check whether it's an empty string. If there's no valid parent ID, we assume this is a parent document (either zero or more children). The parent's key is emitted to the view index. If a document is a child (that is, it has a parentId property), then its key (meta.id) is never indexed, only parentId will be indexed.

The consequence of this view is that all parent documents will appear first, followed immediately by their child tasks (if any). Recall that this ordering is the result of Couchbase sorting the views based on emitted keys. By emitting 0 for the parent and 1 for all children, we guarantee that the parent will always appear first.

To build a page that displays a task with its children listed, we can simply query the view using an array key, where the first element is the parent's ID (or key) and the second element is the number 1 we used to identify children in our map function, as shown next. The following Python snippet omits some details, including the JSON conversions previously shown:

```
@app.route("/tasks/view/<key>", methods=["GET"])
def edit(key):
    parent = client.get(key) #retrieve from the bucket
    children = client.query("tasks", "with_children", key=[key, 1])
    return render_view("view.html",  parent=parent,
children=children)
```

Summary

In this chapter, we walked through the basics of creating a simple Couchbase-backed application. In more complex applications, we need to concern ourselves with advanced tasks, such as locking records with CAS or general design patterns for a particular platform.

What you did learn, however, were the basic building blocks of a Couchbase application. All database-driven applications start with some simple form of CRUD, and grow more complex when the requirements are fleshed out. With the topics covered in this chapter, you'll be able to start building an application with Couchbase.

An important thing to remember about building a Couchbase application is that by virtue of being key/value stores, Couchbase applications tend to be simpler in terms of data management. Effectively, all changes to data occur one-at-a time and by key.

Moreover, documents are retrieved in full and updated in full. There are no partial updates. While this might seem like a limiting feature, it does reduce a fair deal of friction found when working with other data stores, where object mappings are made more complex by joins, projections, and aggregations.

Because Couchbase supports so many programming platforms with its SDKs, it would have been impossible to visit all of them in this chapter's examples. For those who wish to see more complete examples of the code in this chapter, the source for working applications will be available at `https://bitbucket.org/johnzablocki/ couchbase-book`.

Couchbase SDKs

Throughout this book, we explored Couchbase SDKs. This appendix provides more details on obtaining and configuring the most popular Couchbase client libraries. The goal of this section is not to provide comprehensive documentation for each SDK, but rather to aid in your efforts to follow along with the examples in this book.

There are two types of Couchbase client libraries. The first type is the native libraries. These SDKs are written entirely in the language within which they will be used. In this category are the C#, Java, and C libraries. The second type of SDKs are wrappers around the Couchbase C client. These SDKs include Python, Ruby, PHP, and Node.js.

The Couchbase Developer Solutions team maintains the SDKs we just listed. There are other community-maintained clients. However, for the remainder of this appendix, we'll focus only on the official SDKs.

Couchbase Java SDK

The Couchbase Java SDK is a purely Java-based library. It is a highly performant package with support for both synchronous and asynchronous operations. The most recent version contains support for Java 8 and earlier releases.

Current version

This SDK should be used for development against Couchbase Server versions ranging from 2.5 to 3.x. Version 1.2 of the SDK was developed to support the earlier versions of Couchbase Server.

How to obtain it

Java developers will most likely want to use Maven to add the Java SDK to their projects. The package is accessible from Maven Central:

```
<dependencies>
    <dependency>
        <groupId>com.couchbase.client</groupId>
        <artifactId>java-client</artifactId>
        <version>2.0.0</version>
    </dependency>
</dependencies>
```

Additionally, the SDK team publishes the Java binaries, which may be found at `http://docs.couchbase.com/developer/java-2.0/download-links.html`. The source code for the library is available on GitHub at `https://github.com/couchbase/couchbase-java-client`.

The basics

The following snippet demonstrates the basics of using the Couchbase Java SDK:

```
//Configure the cluster
CouchbaseCluster cluster = CouchbaseCluster.create("127.0.0.1");

//Open a bucket connection
Bucket bucket = cluster.openBucket("default");

//Create, and store a JSON document
JsonObject message = JsonObject.create().put("message", "The
    Hello, World!");
JsonDocument document =
    bucket.insert(JsonDocument.create("somekey", message));

//Read the document
JsonDocument savedMessage = bucket.get("somekey");

// Close the bucket connection
cluster.disconnect();
```

Couchbase .NET SDK

The Couchbase .NET SDK is a purely C#-based library. Currently, the latest version is 2.0. This version contains support for .NET 4.5+.

Current version

This SDK should be used for all development purposes against all Couchbase Server versions from 2.5 to 3.x. Version 1.3 of the SDK was developed to support earlier versions of Couchbase Server.

How to obtain it

The .NET developers will most likely want to use NuGet to add the Couchbase .NET SDK to their Visual Studio projects. To install Couchbase SDK 2.0, run the following command in **Package Manager Console**:

```
PM> Install-Package CouchbaseNetClient
```

Additionally, the SDK team publishes the .NET binaries, which can be found at http://docs.couchbase.com/developer/dotnet-2.0/download-links.html. The source code for the library is available on GitHub at https://github.com/couchbase/couchbase-net-client.

The basics

The following snippet demonstrates the basics of using the Couchbase .NET SDK:

```
//Configure the cluster defaulting to "127.0.0.1"
var cluster = new Cluster();

//Open a bucket connection defaulting to "default"
var bucket = cluster.OpenBucket();

//Create, and store a JSON document
var document = new Document<dynamic> {
  Id = "somekey", {
    Content = new { Message = "Hello, World!" };
bucket.Upsert(document);

//Read the document
var savedMessage = bucket.GetDocument<dynamic>("somekey");

// Close the bucket connection
bucket.Dispose();
```

Couchbase PHP SDK

The Couchbase PHP SDK is a PHP library that wraps the Couchbase C SDK. Before installing this library, the C library must be installed.

Current version

Currently, the latest version is 2.0.2. This SDK should be used for all development against Couchbase Server versions from 2.5 to 3.x.

How to obtain it

Linux users will be able to install the PHP SDK with `pecl` as follows:

```
$ pecl install couchbase
```

Additionally, the SDK team publishes Windows binaries, which may be found at `http://docs.couchbase.com/developer/php-2.0/download-links.html`. The source code for the library is available on GitHub at `https://github.com/couchbase/php-ext-couchbase`.

The basics

Here are a few snippets that demonstrate the basics of using the Couchbase PHP SDK:

```php
//Configure the cluster
$cluster = new CouchbaseCluster('http://127.0.0.1:8091');

//Open a bucket connection
$bucket = $cluster->openBucket('default');

// Close the bucket connection
cluster.disconnect();
```

The Couchbase Node.js SDK

The Couchbase Node.js SDK is a Node.js library that wraps the Couchbase C SDK. Before installing this library, the C library must be installed.

Current version

Currently, the latest version is 2.0.2. This SDK should be used for all development against Couchbase Server versions from 2.5 to 3.x.

How to obtain it

The Node.js users will likely wish to use the npm package manager to install the Couchbase Node.js SDK. Windows users must also have `node-gyp` along with Visual C++ 10. Information on installing `node-gyp` is available at `https://github.com/TooTallNate/node-gyp`.

```
$ npm install couchbase
```

Additionally, the SDK team publishes binaries, which may be found at `http://docs.couchbase.com/developer/node-2.0/download-links.html`. The source code for the library is available on GitHub at `https://github.com/couchbase/couchnode`.

The basics

The following snippet demonstrates the basics of using the Couchbase PHP SDK:

```
var couchbase = require('couchbase');
var cluster = new couchbase.Cluster();
var bucket = cluster.openBucket('default');
```

Couchbase Python SDK

The Couchbase Python SDK is a Python library wrapping the Couchbase C SDK. Before installing this library, the C library must be installed.

Current version

Currently, the latest version is 1.2. This SDK should be used for all development against Couchbase Server versions from 2.5 to 3.x.

How to obtain it

Python users can obtain the Couchbase Python SDK through the `pip` package manager as follows:

```
$ pip install couchbase
```

The SDK team publishes binaries, which may be found at `https://pypi.python.org/pypi/couchbase#downloads`. The source code for the library is available on GitHub at `https://github.com/couchbase/couchbase-python-client`.

The basics

The following snippet demonstrates the basics of using the Couchbase PHP SDK:

```
client = Couchbase.connect(bucket='default', host='localhost')
```

Couchbase Ruby SDK

The Couchbase Ruby SDK is a Python library wrapping the Couchbase C SDK. Before installing this library, the C library must be installed.

Current version

Currently, the latest version is 1.3. This SDK should be used for all development against Couchbase Server versions from 2.5 to 3.x.

How to obtain it

Ruby users can find the Couchbase Ruby SDK through the `gem` package manager as follows:

```
$ gem install couchbase
```

The basics

The following snippet demonstrates the basics of using the Couchbase PHP SDK:

```
client = Couchbase.connect(:bucket=>'default', :host=>'localhost')
```

Couchbase C SDK

The Couchbase C client library is the core library for several other libraries. It is an asynchronous, single-threaded SDK using callbacks for all operations. It is available on Windows, Linux, and Mac OS X.

Current version

Currently, the latest version is 2.4.5. This SDK should be used for all development against Couchbase Server versions from 2.5 to 3.x.

How to obtain it

C developers can find instructions on building or obtaining the library at `http://docs.couchbase.com/developer/c-2.4/download-install.html`. Numerous binaries are available at this location.

Index

metadata 108
predictable keys 108-110
RAM 108
unique keys 110

L

Linux
Couchbase, installing on 11
locking, Couchbase 34-37

M

Mac OS X
Couchbase, installing on 12
map functions 43
MapReduce
about 43
basic mapping 45, 46
basic reducing 46, 47
map functions 43
reduce functions 44
mathematical operations
performing 100, 101
Membase 7
Memcached 7
metadata 108
micro framework 130
missing properties 98
model-view-controller (MVC) 129, 130
most recently used (MRU) 23
multiple keys per document 73-75

N

N1QL
about 93
installing 93-95
SDK support 104
nested collections 68-70
nested tasks 139, 140
nginx web server 38
node-gyp
URL 147
NoSQL
landscape 8, 9
taxonomies 10
null properties 98

O

object-relational impedance mismatch 116
Object Relational Mappers (ORM) 7
object schemas 119, 120
object-to-document mappings 116
Open Beer Database 85

P

PersistTo argument 39
ports 12
predictable keys 108-110

Q

querying, by type 67, 68
querying, with beer-sample
about 81
beer documents, finding by brewery 87
breweries, counting by location 83-87
collated views 87-90
documents, querying by type 82, 83

R

RAM
using 23
range query
using 71-73
record
creating 27, 28
deleting 28-30
reading 28-30
updating 27, 28
Redis 107
reduce functions 44
replication 21

S

schema
finalizing 125, 126
schema-less, structure changes 121-123
SDK
clients, using 131
support, for N1QL 104
working with 128

sharding 21
simple queries 96, 97
simple to-do schema 127, 128
string utilities 99, 100

T

task
 creating 132, 133
 listing 133-138
temporary keys 30, 31
to-do app
 about 127
 simple to-do schema 128
transcoder 33

U

unique keys 110

V

values
 emitting 79-81
vBuckets 22
view
 about 42
 creating 55-60
views, querying
 eventual consistency 64
 grouping 62
 key queries 63

W

Windows
 Couchbase, installing on 11

Thank you for buying
Couchbase Essentials

About Packt Publishing

Packt, pronounced 'packed', published its first book, *Mastering phpMyAdmin for Effective MySQL Management*, in April 2004, and subsequently continued to specialize in publishing highly focused books on specific technologies and solutions.

Our books and publications share the experiences of your fellow IT professionals in adapting and customizing today's systems, applications, and frameworks. Our solution-based books give you the knowledge and power to customize the software and technologies you're using to get the job done. Packt books are more specific and less general than the IT books you have seen in the past. Our unique business model allows us to bring you more focused information, giving you more of what you need to know, and less of what you don't.

Packt is a modern yet unique publishing company that focuses on producing quality, cutting-edge books for communities of developers, administrators, and newbies alike. For more information, please visit our website at www.packtpub.com.

About Packt Open Source

In 2010, Packt launched two new brands, Packt Open Source and Packt Enterprise, in order to continue its focus on specialization. This book is part of the Packt Open Source brand, home to books published on software built around open source licenses, and offering information to anybody from advanced developers to budding web designers. The Open Source brand also runs Packt's Open Source Royalty Scheme, by which Packt gives a royalty to each open source project about whose software a book is sold.

Writing for Packt

We welcome all inquiries from people who are interested in authoring. Book proposals should be sent to author@packtpub.com. If your book idea is still at an early stage and you would like to discuss it first before writing a formal book proposal, then please contact us; one of our commissioning editors will get in touch with you.

We're not just looking for published authors; if you have strong technical skills but no writing experience, our experienced editors can help you develop a writing career, or simply get some additional reward for your expertise.

Big Data Analytics with R and Hadoop

ISBN: 978-1-78216-328-2   Paperback: 238 pages

Set up an integrated infrastructure of R and Hadoop to turn your data analytics into Big Data analytics

1. Write Hadoop MapReduce within R.

2. Learn data analytics with R and the Hadoop platform.

3. Handle HDFS data within R.

4. Understand Hadoop streaming with R.

Data Visualization: a successful design process

ISBN: 978-1-84969-346-2   Paperback: 206 pages

A structured design approach to equip you with the knowledge of how to successfully accomplish any data visualization challenge efficiently and effectively

1. A portable, versatile, and flexible data visualization design approach that will help you navigate the complex path towards success.

2. Explains the many different reasons for creating visualizations and identifies the key parameters that lead to very different design options.

3. Thorough explanation of the many visual variables and visualization taxonomy to provide you with a menu of creative options.

Please check **www.PacktPub.com** for information on our titles

Learning Big Data with Amazon Elastic MapReduce

ISBN: 978-1-78217-343-4   Paperback: 242 pages

Easily learn, build, and execute real-world Big Data solutions using Hadoop and AWS EMR

1. Learn how to solve big data problems using Apache Hadoop.

2. Use Amazon Elastic MapReduce to create and maintain cluster infrastructure for big data analytics.

3. A step-by-step guide exploring the vast set of services provided by Amazon on the cloud.

Implementing Splunk: Big Data Reporting and Development for Operational Intelligence

ISBN: 978-1-84969-328-8   Paperback: 448 pages

Learn to transform your machine data into valuable IT and business insights with this comprehensive and practical tutorial

1. Learn to search, dashboard, configure, and deploy Splunk on one machine or thousands.

2. Start working with Splunk fast with a tested set of practical examples and useful advice.

3. Step-by-step instructions and examples with a comprehensive coverage for Splunk veterans and newbies alike.

Please check **www.PacktPub.com** for information on our titles